Masahiro Yagisawa

Fully Homomorphic Encryption on Octonion Ring

Masahiro Yagisawa

Fully Homomorphic Encryption on Octonion Ring

Fully homomorphic encryption with multivariate polynomials on non-associative ring

LAP LAMBERT Academic Publishing

Impressum / Imprint
Bibliografische Information der Deutschen Nationalbibliothek: Die Deutsche Nationalbibliothek verzeichnet diese Publikation in der Deutschen Nationalbibliografie; detaillierte bibliografische Daten sind im Internet über http://dnb.d-nb.de abrufbar.
Alle in diesem Buch genannten Marken und Produktnamen unterliegen warenzeichen-, marken- oder patentrechtlichem Schutz bzw. sind Warenzeichen oder eingetragene Warenzeichen der jeweiligen Inhaber. Die Wiedergabe von Marken, Produktnamen, Gebrauchsnamen, Handelsnamen, Warenbezeichnungen u.s.w. in diesem Werk berechtigt auch ohne besondere Kennzeichnung nicht zu der Annahme, dass solche Namen im Sinne der Warenzeichen- und Markenschutzgesetzgebung als frei zu betrachten wären und daher von jedermann benutzt werden dürften.

Bibliographic information published by the Deutsche Nationalbibliothek: The Deutsche Nationalbibliothek lists this publication in the Deutsche Nationalbibliografie; detailed bibliographic data are available in the Internet at http://dnb.d-nb.de.
Any brand names and product names mentioned in this book are subject to trademark, brand or patent protection and are trademarks or registered trademarks of their respective holders. The use of brand names, product names, common names, trade names, product descriptions etc. even without a particular marking in this work is in no way to be construed to mean that such names may be regarded as unrestricted in respect of trademark and brand protection legislation and could thus be used by anyone.

Coverbild / Cover image: www.ingimage.com

Verlag / Publisher:
LAP LAMBERT Academic Publishing
ist ein Imprint der / is a trademark of
OmniScriptum GmbH & Co. KG
Heinrich-Böcking-Str. 6-8, 66121 Saarbrücken, Deutschland / Germany
Email: info@lap-publishing.com

Herstellung: siehe letzte Seite /
Printed at: see last page
ISBN: 978-3-659-77391-4

PREFACE

Fully homomorphic encryption (FHE) is the cryptographical scheme with both addition and multiplication (thereby based on the ring structure of the plaintexts). Using such a scheme, we can construct the schemes which may be run on encryptions of their inputs to produce an encryption of their output. Since such a scheme does not decrypt its input, it can be run by an untrusted party without revealing its inputs and internal state. The existence of the cryptographical schemes with efficiency and fully homomorphism brings great practical implications in the outsourcing of private computations, for instance, in the context of cloud computing.

FHE is a desirable feature in modern communication system architectures. FHE would allow the chaining together of different services without exposing the data to each of those services. For instance, a chain of different services from different companies could calculate
   1) the tax,
   2) the currency exchange rate,
   3) shipping on a transaction
without exposing the unencrypted data to each of those services.

FHE schemes are malleable by design. The fully homomorphic property of various cryptosystems can be used to create secure voting systems, collision-resistant hash functions, private information retrieval schemes and enable widespread use of cloud computing by ensuring the confidentiality of processed data.

There are several efficient, partially homomorphic cryptosystems, and a number of fully homomorphic, but less efficient cryptosystems. Although a cryptosystem which is unintentionally homomorphic can be subject to attacks on this basis, if treated carefully homomorphism can also be used to perform computations securely.

In 2009 Craig Gentry is creating an encryption system [0.1] that could solve the problem keeping many organizations from using cloud computing to analyze and mine data.

The problem is that while data can be sent to and from a cloud provider's data center in encrypted form, the servers that power a cloud can't do any work on it that way. Gentry has shown that it is possible to analyze data without decrypting it. The key is to encrypt the data in such a way that performing a mathematical operation on the encrypted information and then decrypting the result produces the same answer as performing an analogous operation on the unencrypted data. The correspondence between the operations on unencrypted data and the operations to be performed on encrypted data is known as a **homomorphism**.

It is said that "the problem of how to create true fully homomorphic encryption has been debated for more than 30 years, and Gentry was the first person who got it right and figured out how to make the math work" and "however, because Gentry's scheme with **bootstrapping** technique currently requires a huge amount of computation, there's a long way to go before it will be widely usable".

Gentry's scheme uses a second layer of encryption, essentially to protect intermediate results when the system broke down and needed to be reset. Unfortunately, his scheme requires chaining together thousands of basic operations for finding a piece of text in an e-mail.

Gentry acknowledges that the way he applied the double layer of encryption was "a bit of a hack" and that the system runs too slowly for practical use, but he is working on optimizing it for specific applications such as searching databases for records. He estimates that these applications could be ready for the market in five to 10 years.

It is said that "All known FHE schemes are based on the hardness of lattice problems. Can we construct FHE from other, perhaps number-theoretic assumptions? How about the hardness of factoring or discrete logarithms?".

The fully homomorhic encryption scheme that runs fast for practical use is not proposed until now.

In this book I propose the fully homomorphic encryption scheme on non-associative octonion [0.2] ring over finite field without bootstrapping technique.
In previous work I proposed a fully homomorphic encryption without bootstrapping which has the weak point in the enciphering function [0.3],[0.4],[0.5]. In this book I propose the improved fully homomorphic encryption scheme.
I improve the previous scheme by

(1)   adopting the enciphering function such that it is difficult to express simply by using the matrices,

(2)   constructing the composition of the plaintext p with two sub-plaintexts u and v . The improved scheme is immune from the "p and -p attack".

The improved scheme is based on multivariate algebraic equations with high degree or too many variables while the almost all multivariate cryptosystems proposed until now are based on the quadratic equations for avoiding the explosion of the coefficients. The improved scheme is against the Gröbner basis attack.

The key size of this scheme and complexity for enciphering /deciphering become to be small enough to handle.

To break these cryptosystems it is thought that we probably need to solve the multivariate algebraic equations that are equal to solving the NP complete problem. Then it is thought that these systems are immune from the attacks by the quantum computers.

In chapter 1, the preliminaries for reading later chapters are explained. First, the explanation on a group, ring and field is presented. Second, the mathematical preparation on the octonion ring is explained as the octonion ring is the basic ring of the cryptosystems described in the later chapter. Third, polynomial ring in several variables is mentioned simply. Next the property of the fully homomorphic enciphering and deciphering functions is mentioned. And quantum computer is mentioned which is said to be able to break the RSA cryptosystem based on the problem of factorization synthesis number , the elliptic cryptosystem based on the elliptic curve discrete logarithm problem and so on. At the end of this chapter a simple explanation on Gröbner basis attack is described.

In chapter 2 previous works about fully homomorphic encryption are mentioned.

In chapter 3 two simple examples of fully homomorphic encryption on octonion ring are mentioned.

In chapter 4 proposed fully homomorphic encryption scheme using the multivariate polynomials over the finite field Fq is constructed concretely. This system has the computational difficulty to solve the multivariate algebraic equations over the finite field Fq that is equal to solving the NP complete problem. At the beginning the summary is placed. Preliminaries for octonion operation are described for the understanding of the readers. In the next we describe the concept of proposed fully homomorphic encryption scheme.

At end o f chapter 4 the conceptual charts of the additional circuit and multiplicative circuit of ciphertexts in the proposed fully homomorphic encryption sheme are attached.

A bibliography is provided after chapter 4.

Finally appendix A, B, C and D are attached.

Chapters are divided into Sections, which are numbered chapter-wise. Chapter 4 has the summary at the beginning of the chapter and the conclusion remarks at the end of the chapter. The equation number (c.e) refers to the e-th equation in chapter c.

I typed the manuscript with utmost care, but some oversight or discrepancy is thought to exist yet. I shall acknowledge thankfully the oversight or discrepancy brought to the notice by inquisitive readers.

I wish to accord here my warm gratitude to the publisher (Lambert Academic, Germany) for kindly providing an opportunity to accomplish the task.

Finally I would like to thank my wife, *Momoe,* for supporting me mentally through writing this book. I would like to dedicate this book to her.

Yokohama (Japan): (August 19, 2015)   Masahiro Yagisawa

CONTENTS

CHAPTER 1

PRELIMINARIES

§1. Group, ring and field

We explain a *group,* a *ring*, and a *field* simply.

A *group* is a set of elements, together with an operation performed on pairs of these elements such that,

1) When two elements of the set as arguments are given, the operation always returns an element of the set as its result. It is thus fully defined, and closed over the set.

2) One element of the set is an identity element. Thus, let $\otimes$ be the operation. There is some element of the set e such that for any other element of the set x,

$$e \otimes x = x \otimes e = x.$$

3) Every element of the set has an inverse element. Let p be any element of the set. Then there is another element q such that

$$p \otimes q = q \otimes p = e.$$

4) The operation $\otimes$ is associative. That is, for any three elements of the set,

$$(a \otimes b) \otimes c = a \otimes (b \otimes c).$$

There are many different kinds of finite *groups*, in which there are some *groups* with very complex structure. Most *groups* belong to families of *groups* with an infinite number of members. Thus, addition modulo 5 yields the cyclic *group* of order 5, and there are cyclic *groups* of every integer order starting with 2.

A *ring* is a set of elements with two operations. Let + be the one operation to be like addition, and let * be the other to be like multiplication. The operations have the following properties:

1) The elements of the *ring*, together with the addition operation, form a *group*.
2) Addition is commutative. That is, for any two elements of the set p and q,
$$p + q = q + p.$$
3) The multiplication operation is associative in general. (But the octonion ring

described later has non-associative property.)

4) Multiplication distributes over addition: that is, for any three elements of the *group* a, b and c,

$$a * (b + c) = (a * b) + (a * c).$$

For example, addition and multiplication modulo 5 yield *rings*. Matrix multiplication also leads to *rings* as well.

A *field* is a *ring* in which the elements, other than the identity element for addition, and the multiplication operator, also form a *group*.

There are only two kinds of finite *fields* denoted by Fq. One kind is the *field* formed by addition and multiplication modulo a prime number. The other kind of finite *field* has a number of elements that is a power of a prime number. The addition operator consists of multiple independent additions modulo that prime. The elements of the *field* can be thought of as polynomials whose coefficients are numbers modulo that prime. In that case, multiplication is polynomial multiplication, where not only the coefficients are modulo that prime, but the polynomials are modulo a special kind of polynomial, known as a primitive polynomial. All finite *fields*, but particularly those of this second kind, are known as *Galois fields*.

§2. Octonion ring over *Fq*

Let q be a prime larger than 2.
    Let O be the octonion ring over Fq. Every element of O can be written as a linear combination of these basis elements 1, e_1, ..., e_7.
    That is,

$$c_0 1 + c_1 e_1 + c_2 e_2 + c_3 e_3 + c_4 e_4 + c_5 e_5 + c_6 e_6 + c_7 e_7 \text{ where } c_0,...,c_7 \in Fq.$$

The basis element 1 will be the identity element of O, meaning that multiplication by 1 does nothing, and for this reason, elements of O are usually written

$$c_0 + c_1 e_1 + c_2 e_2 + c_3 e_3 + c_4 e_4 + c_5 e_5 + c_6 e_6 + c_7 e_7,$$

suppressing the basis element 1. When this basis is given, non-associative octonion multiplication is defined by first defining the products of basis elements and then defining all other products using the distributive law.

If we select 2 as q, the multiplication between the two or three elements of $\boldsymbol{O}$ has not the non-commutative and non-associative property. Then, in this book we don't adopt 2 as q.

We mention multiplication of basis elements as follows.

When multiplying octonions, there are rules for combining the different imaginary operators. The multiplication rules can be shown by the 'fano plane' (see **Fig.1.1**).

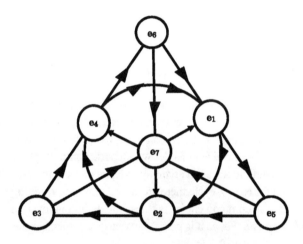

Fig.1.1 fano plane

It works as follows, if you want to multiply e_3 by e_7 for example, look at the diagram and find the line that joins them and you will see that there is a third point on the line, in this case $\mathbf{e_1}$. Following the arrows, you go from $\mathbf{e_3}$ to $\mathbf{e_7}$ to $\mathbf{e_1}$ so $\mathbf{e_3}\,\mathbf{e_7} = \mathbf{e_1}$ reversing the order of the multiplicands gives minus the result so if the order on the line is reversed then put a negative sign in front of the result.

The square of any imaginary operator is **-1** such that

$$e_1{}^2=e_2{}^2=e_3{}^2=e_4{}^2=e_5{}^2=e_6{}^2=e_7{}^2= \textbf{-1}$$

where e_i ($i=1,\ldots,7$) are basis elements of $\boldsymbol{O}$, and all the possible products of e_i and e_j($i,j=1,\ldots,7$) are determined.

Table 1.1 Multiplication table for octonions

	1	e_1	e_2	e_3	e_4	e_5	e_6	e_7
1	1	e_1	e_2	e_3	e_4	e_5	e_6	e_7
e_1	e_1	-1	e_4	e_7	$-e_2$	e_6	$-e_5$	$-e_3$
e_2	e_2	$-e_4$	-1	e_5	e_1	$-e_3$	e_7	$-e_6$
e_3	e_3	$-e_7$	$-e_5$	-1	e_6	e_2	$-e_4$	e_1
e_4	e_4	e_2	$-e_1$	$-e_6$	-1	e_7	e_3	$-e_5$
e_5	e_5	$-e_6$	e_3	$-e_2$	$-e_7$	-1	e_1	e_4
e_6	e_6	e_5	$-e_7$	e_4	$-e_3$	$-e_1$	-1	e_2
e_7	e_7	e_3	e_6	$-e_1$	e_5	$-e_4$	$-e_2$	-1

The above definition is not unique, but is only one of 480 possible definitions for octonion multiplication with $e_0 = 1$. The others can be obtained by permuting and changing the signs of the non-scalar basis elements. The 480 different algebras are isomorphic, and there is rarely a need to consider which particular multiplication rule is used. Each of these 480 definitions is invariant up to signs under some 7-cycle of the points (1234567), and for each 7-cycle there are four definitions, differing by signs and reversal of order. A common choice is to use the definition invariant under the 7-cycle (1234567) with $e_1e_2 = e_4$ as it is particularly easy to remember the multiplication.

Here I show some examples of the multiplication. From **table1.1** we obtain

$$(((((e_1e_2)e_3)e_4)e_5)e_6 = (((e_4e_3)e_4)e_5)e_6 = ((-e_6e_4)e_5)e_6 = (-(-e_3e_5))e_6 = -(-e_2e_6) = -(-e_7) = e_7.$$

The other products can be determined by similar methods, resulting in

$$((((e_2e_3)e_4)e_5)e_6)e_7 = (((e_5e_4)e_5)e_6)e_7 = ((-e_7e_5)e_6)e_7 = (-(-e_4e_6))e_7 = -(-e_3e_7) = -(-e_1) = e_1,$$

$$((((e_3e_4)e_5)e_6)e_7)e_1 = (((e_6e_5)e_6)e_7)e_1 = ((-e_1e_6)e_7)e_1 = (-(-e_5e_7))e_1 = -(-e_4e_1) = -(-e_2) = e_2,$$

$$\ldots \quad \ldots \quad \ldots \quad \ldots$$

$$((((e_7e_1)e_2)e_3)e_4)e_5 = (((e_3e_2)e_3)e_4)e_5 = ((-e_5e_3)e_4)e_5 = (-(-e_2e_4))e_5 = -(-e_1e_5) = -(-e_6) = e_6.$$

For two elements

$$a = a_0 + a_1e_1 + a_2e_2 + a_3e_3 + a_4e_4 + a_5e_5 + a_6e_6 + a_7e_7$$

and

$$b = b_0 + b_1 e_1 + b_2e_2 + b_3e_3 + b_4e_4 + b_5e_5 + b_6e_6 + b_7e_7,$$

addition $a+b$ mod q is determined as follows.

$a+b$ mod q

$$:= a_0 + a_1e_1 + a_2e_2 + a_3e_3 + a_4e_4 + a_5e_5 + a_6e_6 + a_7e_7 + b_0 + b_1 e_1 + b_2e_2 + b_3e_3 + b_4e_4 + b_5e_5 + b_6e_6 + b_7e_7$$

$$= (a_0 + b_0 \bmod q) + (a_1+b_1 \bmod q)e_1 + (a_2+b_2 \bmod q)e_2 + (a_3+b_3 \bmod q)e_3$$

$$+ (a_4+b_4 \bmod q)e_4 + (a_5+b_5 \bmod q)e_5 + (a_6+b_6 \bmod q)e_6 + (a_7+b_7 \bmod q)e_7.$$

Their product ab is determined by the products of the basis elements and the distributive low. The distributive law makes it possible to expand the product so that it is a sum of products of basis elements. This gives the following expression:

ab mod q

$$:= (a_0 + a_1e_1 + a_2e_2 + a_3e_3 + a_4e_4 + a_5e_5 + a_6e_6 + a_7e_7)(b_0 + b_1 e_1 + b_2e_2 + b_3e_3 + b_4e_4 + b_5e_5 + b_6e_6 + b_7e_7).$$

Now the basis elements can be multiplied using the rules given above to get

$$= (a_0b_0 - a_1b_1 - a_2b_2 - a_3b_3 - a_4b_4 - a_5b_5 - a_6b_6 - a_7b_7 \bmod q)$$

$$+ (a_0b_1 + a_1b_0 + a_2b_4 + a_3b_7 - a_4b_2 + a_5b_6 - a_6b_5 - a_7b_3 \bmod q)\, e_1$$

$$+ (a_0b_2 - a_1b_4 + a_2b_0 + a_3b_5 + a_4b_1 - a_5b_3 + a_6b_7 - a_7b_6 \bmod q)\, e_2,$$

$$+ (a_0b_3 - a_1b_7 - a_2b_5 + a_3b_0 + a_4b_6 + a_5b_2 - a_6b_4 + a_7b_1 \bmod q)\, e_3$$

$$+ (a_0b_4 + a_1b_2 - a_2b_1 - a_3b_6 + a_4b_0 + a_5b_7 + a_6b_3 - a_7b_5 \bmod q)\, e_4$$

$$+ (a_0b_5 - a_1b_6 + a_2b_3 - a_3b_2 - a_4b_7 + a_5b_0 + a_6b_1 + a_7b_4 \bmod q)\, e_5$$

$$+ (a_0b_6 + a_1b_5 - a_2b_7 + a_3b_4 - a_4b_3 - a_5b_1 + a_6b_0 + a_7b_2 \bmod q)\, e_6$$

$$+(a_0b_7+a_1b_3+a_2b_6-a_3b_1+a_4b_5-a_5b_4-a_6b_2+a_7b_0 \bmod q)\, e_7.$$

We define ordered list form which we call the element expression as follows. Using the basis $\mathbf{1}$, e_i (i=1,…,7) of $\mathbf{O}$ makes it possible to write $\mathbf{O}$ as a set of octuple (8-tuple):

$$\mathbf{O}=\{(a_0,a_1,a_2,a_3,a_4,a_5,a_6,a_7)/a_i\in \mathbf{Fq}(i{=}0,\ldots,7)\ \}.$$

Then the basis elements $\mathbf{1}$, e_i (i=1,…,7) correspond to (1,0,0,0,0,0,0,0), (0,1,0,0,0,0,0,0), (0,0,1,0,0,0,0,0), (0,0,0,1,0,0,0,0), (0,0,0,0,1,0,0,0), (0,0,0,0,0,1,0,0), (0,0,0,0,0,0,1,0) and (0,0,0,0,0,0,0,1).

In general multiplication of $\mathbf{a}$=(a_0,a_1,a_2,a_3,…, a_7) and $\mathbf{b}$=(b_0,b_1,b_2,b_3,…,b_7) is non-commutative.
$\mathbf{b}$ is commutative to given $\mathbf{a}$ under the condition that

$$a_ib_j{-}a_jb_i\bmod q = 0\ (i{<}j;\ i,j{=}1,\ldots,7).$$

That is, $\mathbf{b}$ to be commutative to $\mathbf{a}$ is given as follows.

$$\mathbf{b}{=}(b_0,\ ra_1,\ ra_2,\ ra_3,\ldots,ra_7),$$

where

$$r\in \mathbf{Fq}.$$

At **CHAPTER 3** and **CHAPTER 4** **§ 2. Preliminaries for octonion operation** we describe the property of octonion such as non-associativity A, B and $C\in \mathbf{O}$

$$(AB)C{\neq}A(BC) \bmod q\ \in \mathbf{O}$$

and so on.

§3. Polynomial ring over octonion ring in several variables

A polynomial P in n variables $X_1,\ldots,X_n$ with coefficients in a ring O is defined as follows. For any multi-index $a = (a_0,\ldots,a_{n-1})$, where each a_i is a non-negative integer, let

$$X^a := \prod_{i=0}^{n-1} X_i^{a_i} = X_0^{a_0} X_1^{a_1} \ldots X_{n-1}^{a_{n-1}},$$

$$P_a := P_{a_0 a_1 \ldots a_{n-1}} \in O.$$

The product X^a is called the monomial of multi-degree a. A polynomial P is a finite linear combination of monomials with coefficients in O such that

$$P := \sum_a P_a X^a$$

and finitely many coefficients P_a are different from 0. The degree of a monomial X^a, frequently denoted $|a|$, is defined as

$$|a| := \sum_{i=0}^{n-1} a_i,$$

and the degree of a polynomial P is the largest degree of a monomial occurring with non-zero coefficient in the expansion of P. Polynomials P in n variables with coefficients in O form a non-commutative ring denoted $O[X_0,\ldots,X_{n-1}]$, or sometimes $O[X]$, where X is a symbol representing the full set of variables, $X = (X_0,\ldots,X_{n-1})$, and called the polynomial ring in n variables.

As an example, we notice the following polynomials.

$$F(X) := A_1(A_2(\ldots(A_k X)\ldots)) \bmod q \in O[X],$$

where

$A_i \in O$ is the coefficients $(i=1,\ldots,k)$ and $X = (x_0,\ldots,x_7) \in O$ is a variable,

$F(X)$ has the element expression as follows.

$$F(X) = A_1(A_2(\ldots(A_k X)\ldots)),$$

$$=(\ a_{00}x_0+a_{01}x_1+...+a_{07}x_7,$$

$$a_{10}x_0+a_{11}x_1+...+a_{17}x_7,$$

$$...\quad ...\quad ...$$

$$a_{70}x_0+a_{71}x_1+...+a_{77}x_7\ )\ \mathrm{mod}\ q$$

with $a_{ij}\in Fq\ (i,j=0,...,7)$.

When $X=M=(m_0,...,m_7)\in O$, $F(M)$ is given such that

$$F(M)=A_1(A_2(...(A_kM)...)),$$

$$=(\ a_{00}m_0+a_{01}m_1+...+a_{07}m_7,$$

$$a_{10}m_0+a_{11}m_1+...+a_{17}m_7,$$

$$...\quad ...\quad ...$$

$$a_{70}m_0+a_{71}m_1+...+a_{77}m_7\ )\ \mathrm{mod}\ q$$

Let $(f_0,...,f_7):=F(M)$.

We can calculate $m_0,...,m_6$ and m_7 from $f_0,...,f_6$ and f_7 as follows.

$$a_{00}m_0+a_{01}m_1+...+a_{07}m_7\ \mathrm{mod}\ q=f_0$$

$$a_{10}m_0+a_{11}m_1+...+a_{17}m_7\ \mathrm{mod}\ q=f_1$$

$$...\quad ...\quad ...$$

$$a_{70}m_0+a_{71}m_1+...+a_{77}m_7\ \mathrm{mod}\ q=f_7$$

where $\det(a_{ij})\neq 0\ \mathrm{mod}\ q$.

We solve the above simultaneous equation to obtain $m_0,...,m_6$ and m_7.

Next let $F(G(X))\in O[X]$ or $G(F(X))\in O[X]$ be the composite function of $F(X)\in O[X]$ and $G(X)\in O[X]$

where

$$F(X)=A_1(A_2(...(A_kX)...)),$$

$$=(\,a_{00}x_0+a_{01}x_1+\ldots+a_{07}x_7,$$

$$a_{10}x_0+a_{11}x_1+\ldots+a_{17}x_7,$$

$$\ldots \qquad \ldots \qquad \ldots$$

$$a_{70}x_0+a_{71}x_1+\ldots+a_{77}x_7\,)\bmod q,$$

$A_i \in O(i=1,\ldots,k)$ are the coefficients of $F(X)$,

and

$$G(X)=B_1(B_2(\ldots(B_hX)\ldots),$$

$$=(\,b_{00}x_0+b_{01}x_1+\ldots+b_{07}x_7,$$

$$b_{10}x_0+b_{11}x_1+\ldots+b_{17}x_7,$$

$$\ldots \qquad \ldots \qquad \ldots$$

$$b_{70}x_0+b_{71}x_1+\ldots+b_{77}x_7)\bmod q$$

with $a_{ij}\in Fq(i,j=0,\ldots,7)$.

$B_i \in O(i=1,\ldots,h)$ is the coefficient of $G(X)$.

$F(G(X)) \in O[X]$ is obtained as follows.

$F(G(X))= A_1(A_2(\ldots(A_k(B_1(B_2(\ldots(B_hX)\ldots)\bmod q,$

$=(\,a_{00}(b_{00}x_0+b_{01}x_1+\ldots+b_{07}x_7)+a_{01}(b_{10}x_0+b_{11}x_1+\ldots+b_{17}x_7)+\ldots+a_{07}(b_{70}x_0+b_{71}x_1+\ldots+b_{77}x_7),$

$a_{10}(b_{00}x_0+b_{01}x_1+\ldots+b_{07}x_7)+a_{11}(b_{10}x_0+b_{11}x_1+\ldots+b_{17}x_7)+\ldots+a_{17}(b_{70}x_0+b_{71}x_1+\ldots+b_{77}x_7),$

$$\ldots \qquad \ldots \qquad \ldots$$

$a_{70}(b_{00}x_0+b_{01}x_1+\ldots+b_{07}x_7)+a_{71}(b_{10}x_0+b_{11}x_1+\ldots+b_{17}x_7)+\ldots+a_{77}(b_{70}x_0+b_{71}x_1+\ldots+b_{77}x_7))\bmod q$

$=((a_{00}b_{00}+a_{01}b_{10}+\ldots+a_{07}b_{70})x_0+(\,a_{00}b_{01}+a_{01}b_{11}+\ldots+a_{07}b_{71})x_1+\ldots+(a_{00}b_{07}+a_{01}b_{17}+\ldots+a_{07}b_{77})\,x_7,$

$(a_{10}b_{00}+a_{11}b_{10}+\ldots+a_{17}b_{70})x_0+(\,a_{10}b_{01}+a_{11}b_{11}+\ldots+a_{17}b_{71})x_1+\ldots+(a_{10}b_{07}+a_{11}b_{17}+\ldots+a_{17}b_{77})\,x_7,$

$$\ldots \qquad \ldots \qquad \ldots$$

$(a_{70}b_{00}+ a_{71}b_{10}+\ldots+ a_{77}b_{70})x_0+(a_{70}b_{01}+ a_{71}\,b_{11}+\ldots+a_{77}b_{71})x_1+\ldots +(a_{70}b_{07}+ a_{71}b_{17}+\ldots+ a_{77}b_{77})\,x_7)$ mod q.

Since multiplication on octonoin ring has the property of non-commutative and non-associative, we notice the following property of the polynomials on octonion ring.

Let

$$K(X):=C_1(C_2X)) \text{ mod } q \in O[X],$$

$$H(X,Y):= D_1(Y(D_2X) \text{ mod } q \in O[X,Y],$$

and

$$E(X,Y):=D_1(C_1(C_2(Y(D_2X))) \text{ mod } q \in O[X,Y],$$

where

$C_1,C_2,D_1,D_2 \in O$ are the coefficients and $X= (x_0,\ldots, x_7) \in O[X]$, $Y= (y_0,\ldots, y_7) \in O[Y]$ are symbols representing the full set of variables and D_1 has the inverse $D_1^{-1} \in O$.

$$H(X, K(Y))= D_1(K(Y)\,(D_2X)) \text{ mod } q$$

$$= D_1(\,[C_1(C_2Y)]\,(D_2X)) \text{ mod } q.$$

When $X=Y=1$, we obtain

$$H(X, K(Y)) = D_1(\,[C_1(C_21)]\,(D_21)) \text{ mod } q$$

$$= D_1([C_1C_2]D_2) \text{ mod } q,$$

$$E(X,\ Y) =D_1(C_1(C_2(1\,(D_21))) \text{ mod } q$$

$$= D_1(C_1(C_2D_2)) \text{ mod } q.$$

In general from non-associative property,

$$(C_1C_2)D_2 \neq C_1(C_2D_2) \text{ mod } q.$$

Left-multiplying both sides by D_1 gives

$$D_1(\,(C_1C_2)D_2) \neq D_1(C_1(C_2D_2)) \bmod q.$$

Then we have

$$H(X,\,K(Y)) \neq E(X,Y) \bmod q.$$

§4. Fully homomorphic enciphering/deciphering function (FHEDF)

FHEDF has the following property (in its simplest form). Ciphertexts c_i are deciphered to plaintexts m_i, i.e., Decrypt$(c_i) = m_i$, where the m_i's and c_i's are elements of some ring (with two operations, addition and multiplication). In fully homomorphic encryption (FHE) we have the expression such that

$$\text{Decrypt } (c_1 + c_2) = m_1 + m_2; \text{ Decrypt } (c_1 {*} c_2) = m_1 {*} m_2:$$

In other words, decryption is doubly homomorphic, i.e., homomorphic with respect to the two operations addition and multiplication.

Being fully homomorphic means that whenever f is a function composed of (finitely many) additions and multiplications in the ring, then

$$\text{Decrypt } (f(c_1,\ldots, c_t)) = f(m_1,\ldots,m_t):$$

If the cloud (or an adversary) can efficiently compute $f(c_1,\ldots, c_t)$ from ciphertexts $c_1,\ldots, c_t$, without learning any information about the corresponding plaintexts $m_1,\ldots,m_t$ then the system is efficient and secure.

Another requirement for FHEDF is that the ciphertext sizes remain bounded, independent of the function f; this is known as the "compact ciphertexts" requirement. (Depending on the filly homomorphic encryption systems, the messages and ciphertexts could in fact lie in different rings, and multiplication might be accomplished using a tensoring operation.)

Fully homomorphic encryption schemes belong to either public key cryptosystem (where the encryptor knows the decryptor's public key but not her private key) or symmetric key cryptosystem (where the encryptor and decryptor share a key that is used for both encryption and decryption). Fully homomorphic encryption scheme described in chapter 4 belongs to symmetric key cryptosystem. I will describe the new fully homomorphic encryption scheme to belong to public key cryptosystem in near future.

§5. Quantum computer

The principal of a quantum computer is based on quantum mechanical phenomena, such as superposition and entanglement. Quantum computers are different from von Neumann –type computers based on transistors. The basic principle behind quantum computation is that quantum properties can be used to represent data and perform operations on these data. The research is carried out in which quantum computational operations were executed on a very small number of qubits (quantum bits).

If large-scale quantum computers can be built, they will be able to solve certain problems much faster than any classical computer using the best currently known algorithms, for example, integer factorization using Shor's algorithm. Furthermore, there exist quantum algorithms, such as Simon's algorithm, which runs exponentially faster than any possible probabilistic classical algorithm.

It is said that the problem of factoring large integers, the problem of solving discrete logarithms and the problem of computing elliptic curve discrete logarithms are efficiently solved in a polynomial time by the quantum computers.

It is thought that the multivariate public key cryptosystem (MPKC) is immune from the attack of quantum computers because we probably need to solve the multivariate algebraic equations of high degree that is equal to solving the NP complete problem. Then it is thought that the cryptosystem proposed in chapter 4 is immune from the attacks by quantum computers.

§6. Gröbner basis attack

A Gröbner basis [1.1] is a set of multivariate polynomials that has desirable algorithmic properties. Every set of polynomials can be transformed into a Gröbner basis. A Gröbner basis is used to solve a system of polynomial. In the cryptography we can use Gröbner basis to break the public key cryptosystems based on the multivariate polynomials. It is what is called the Gröbner basis attack.

CHAPTER 2

PREVIOUS FULLY HOMOMORPHIC ENCRYPTION SCHEMES

The fully homomorphic encryption scheme has long been something of a Holy Grail for computer scientists. Craig Gentry's recent solution to the problem [0.1], while not efficient enough to be practical, was considered to be a major breakthrough. Then, much progress has been made in the direction of finding efficient **fully homomorphic encryption** (FHE) schemes.

   A major application of FHE is to cloud computing system. User A can store his data in "the cloud", for example, on remote servers that he accesses via the Internet. The cloud has more storage capabilities and computing power than does user A. So when user A needs computations to be done on his data, user A would like those computations to be done by the cloud. However, user A doesn't trust the cloud. His data might be sensitive (for example, user A might be a hospital and the data might be patients' medical records), and user A would like the cloud to know as little as possible about his data, and about the results of the computations. So user A sends encrypted data to the cloud, which can perform arithmetic operations on it without learning anything about the original raw data, by performing operations on the encrypted data.

   Here for reader's understanding we show the survey of the fully homomorphic encryption below.

   The utility of fully homomorphic encryption has been long recognized. The problem of constructing such a scheme was first proposed within a year of the development of RSA [2.1]. For more than 30 years, it was unclear whether fully homomorphic encryption was possible. During this period, the best result was the Boneh-Goh-Nissim cryptosystem which supports evaluation of an unlimited number of addition operations but at most one multiplication.

   Craig Gentry [0.1] using lattice-based cryptosystem showed the first fully homomorphic encryption scheme as announced by IBM on June 25, 2009 [2.2][2.3]. His scheme supports evaluations of arbitrary depth circuits. His construction starts from a somewhat homomorphic encryption scheme using ideal lattices that is limited to evaluating low-degree polynomials over encrypted data. (It is limited because each ciphertext is noisy in some sense, and this noise grows as one adds and multiplies ciphertexts, until ultimately the noise makes the resulting ciphertext indecipherable.) He then shows how to modify this scheme to make it bootstrappable—in particular, he shows that by modifying the somewhat homomorphic scheme slightly, it can actually evaluate its own decryption circuit, a self-referential property. Finally, he shows that any bootstrappable somewhat homomorphic encryption scheme can be converted into a fully homomorphic encryption through a recursive self-embedding.

However, the scheme is impractical for many applications, because ciphertext size and computation time increase sharply as one increases the security level. (Let k be the security parameter.) To obtain 2^k security against known attacks, the computation time and ciphertext size are high-degree polynomials in k.

In 2010, Stehle and Steinfeld reduced the dependence on k substantially [2.4]. They presented optimizations that permit the computation to be only quasi-$k^{3.5}$ per boolean gate of the function being evaluated.

Gentry's Ph.D. thesis [2.5] provides additional details. Gentry also published a high-level overview of the van Dijk et al. construction (described below) in the March 2010 issue of Communications of the ACM [2.6].

In 2009, Marten van Dijk, Craig Gentry, Shai Halevi and Vinod Vaikuntanathan presented a second fully homomorphic encryption scheme [2.7], which uses many of the tools of Gentry's construction, but which does not require ideal lattices. Instead, they show that the somewhat homomorphic component of Gentry's ideal lattice-based scheme can be replaced with a very simple somewhat homomorphic scheme that uses integers. The scheme is therefore conceptually simpler than Gentry's ideal lattice scheme, but has similar properties with regards to homomorphic operations and efficiency. The somewhat homomorphic component in the work of van Dijk et al. is similar to an encryption scheme proposed by Levieil and Naccache in 2008, and also to one that was proposed by Bram Cohen in 1998[2.8]. Cohen's method is not even additively homomorphic, however. The Levieil-Naccache scheme is additively homomorphic, and can be modified to support also a small number of multiplications.

In 2011, Coron, Naccache and Tibouchi proposed a technique allowing to reduce the public-key size $O(\lambda^{10})$ of the van Dijk et al. scheme to $O(\lambda^7)$ [2.9].

In April 2013 the HElib was released, via GitHub, to the open source community which "implements the Brakerski-Gentry- Vaikuntanathan (BGV) homomorphic encryption scheme, along with many optimizations to make homomorphic evaluation runs faster" [2.10].

Recently, Nuida and Kurosawa proposed (batch) fully homomorphic encryption over integers [2.11].

The fully homomorphic encryptions described above have the large complexity for enciphering/deciphering. In chapter 4, I describe the fully homomorphic encryption scheme based on the octonion ring over Fq which have the non-associative and non-commutative property. That is, the scheme has additively homomorphic and multiplicative homomorphic property.

CHAPTER 3

EXAMPLES OF FULLY HOMOMORPHIC ENCIPHERING

FUNCTION ON OCTONION RING O

In this chapter I describe two example of fully homomorphic enciphering functions which are adopted in chapter 4.

§1. Example 1

Let q be a prime more than 2.

Let $M_i=(m_{i0},m_{i1},\ldots,m_{i7}) \in O$ be the plaintext to be encrypted .(i=1,2)

Let $X=(x_0,\ldots,x_7) \in O[X]$ be a variable.

Let $E(Y, X)$ be a enciphering function of user A.

Let $E(M_i,X) \in O[X]$ be the ciphertext. (i=1,2)

$A_i \in O$ is selected randomly such that A_i^{-1} exists (i=1,...,k) which is the secret keys of user A.

$E(Y,X)$ is defined as follows.

$$E(Y,X):=A_1((\ldots((A_k((Y[(A_k^{-1}((\ldots((A_1^{-1}X)Z_1))\ldots))Z_k])Z_k^{-1}))\ldots))Z_1^{-1}) \bmod q \in O[X]$$

$$=(e_{000}x_0\,y_0+e_{001}\,x_0y_1+ \ldots +e_{077}\,x_7y_7,$$

$$e_{100}x_0\,y_0+e_{101}\,x_0y_1+ \ldots +e_{177}\,x_7y_7,$$

$$\ldots \qquad \ldots$$

$$e_{700}x_0\,y_0+e_{701}\,x_0y_1+ \ldots +e_{777}\,x_7y_7,),$$

$$= \{e_{ijk}\}(i,j,k=0,\ldots,7)$$

with $e_{ijk}\in Fq$ (i,j,k =0,...,7) which is published in cloud centre.

[Addition of $E(M_1,X)$ and $E(M_2,X)$]

$$E(M_1,X) \pm E(M_2,X) \bmod q$$

$$= A_1((\ldots((A_k((M_1\,[(A_k^{-1}((\ldots((A_1^{-1}X)Z_1))\ldots))Z_k])Z_k^{-1}))\ldots))Z_1^{-1})+ A_1((\ldots((A_k((M_2\,[(A_k^{-1}((\ldots((A_1^{-1}X)Z_1))\ldots))Z_k])Z_k^{-1}))\ldots))Z_1^{-1}) \bmod q$$

$$= A_1((\ldots((A_k(([M_1 \pm M_2][(A_k^{-1}((\ldots((A_1^{-1}X)Z_1))\ldots))Z_k])Z_k^{-1}))\ldots))Z_1^{-1}) \bmod q.$$

That is,

$$E(M_1, X) \pm E(M_2, X) = E(M_1 \pm M_2, X) \bmod q.$$

[Multiplication of $E(M_1, X)$ and $E(M_2, X)$]

$$E(M_1, E(M_2, X)) \bmod q$$

$$= A_1((\ldots((A_k((M_1 [(A_k^{-1}((\ldots((A_1^{-1}[A_1((\ldots((A_k((M_2 [(A_k^{-1}((\ldots((A_1^{-1}X)Z_1))\ldots))Z_k])$$
$$Z_k^{-1}))\ldots))Z_1^{-1})])Z_1))\ldots))Z_k])Z_k^{-1}))\ldots))Z_1^{-1}) \bmod q$$

$$= A_1((\ldots((A_k((M_1 (M_2 [(A_k^{-1}((\ldots((A_1^{-1}X)Z_1))\ldots))Z_k])Z_k^{-1}))\ldots))Z_1^{-1}) \bmod q$$

We can obtain the plaintext $(M_1 M_2)$ by deciphering as follws.

$$D := A_k^{-1}(\ldots(A_1^{-1}(E(M_1, E(M_2, X))\ldots) \text{ at } X = A_1(\ldots(A_k \mathbf{1})\ldots) \bmod q$$

$$= A_k^{-1}(\ldots(A_1^{-1}(A_1(\ldots(A_k(M_1 (M_2 (A_k^{-1} (\ldots(A_1^{-1}(A_1(\ldots(A_k \mathbf{1})\ldots))\ldots) \bmod q$$

$$= M_1 (M_2 (\mathbf{1})) \bmod q$$

$$= M_1 M_2 \bmod q.$$

§2. Example 2

We also use the same definition of q, A_i, $X = (x_0, \ldots, x_7)$ and $E(M_i, X)$ as example 1.
Here we define the medium text M as follows.
We select the element $B = (b_0, b_1, b_2, \ldots, b_7)$ and $H = (b_0, -b_1, -b_2, \ldots, -b_7) \in O$ such that,

$$L_B := |B|^2 = b_0^2 + b_1^2 + \ldots + b_7^2 \bmod q = 0 \in Fq,$$

$$b_0 \neq 0 \bmod q \in Fq,$$

$$b_1 \neq 0 \bmod q \in Fq.$$

Then we have

$$L_H := |H|^2 = b_0^2 + b_1^2 + \ldots + b_7^2 \bmod q = 0 \in Fq,$$

$$B + H = 2b_0 \mathbf{1} \bmod q,$$

$$B^2 = 2b_0 B \bmod q,$$

$$H^2 = 2b_0 H \bmod q,$$

$$BH = HB = \mathbf{0} \bmod q.$$

Let $u, v \in \boldsymbol{Fq}$ be sub-plaintexts where a plaintext p is given such as

$$p := u + 2b_0 v \bmod q.$$

Let $w \in Fq$ be a random number.
We define the medium text M by

$$M := R_1(\ldots(R_r(u\mathbf{1} + vB + wH)R_r^{-1})\ldots)R_1^{-1} \in O,$$

where

$$p = u + 2b_0 v \bmod q,$$

$R_i \in O$ is selected such that $R_i^{-1} \in O$ exists $(i=1,\ldots,r)$ and

$$R_i B \neq B R_i \bmod q (i=1,\ldots,r),$$

$$R_i H \neq H_i \bmod q (i=1,\ldots,r).$$

Then

$$|M|^2 = |R_1(\ldots(R_r(u\mathbf{1} + vB + wH)R_r^{-1})\ldots)R_1^{-1}|^2$$

$$= (u + b_0(v+w))^2 + (v-w)^2(b_0^2 + b_1^2 + \ldots + b_7^2) \bmod q,$$

$$= (u + b_0(v+w))^2 - (v-w)^2 b_0^2 \bmod q,$$

$$= (u + 2b_0 v)(u + 2b_0 w) \bmod q.$$

Here we simplify the expression of medium text M such that

$$M := R(u + vB + wH)R^{-1} \in O.$$

Let $u_i \in Fq$ be the plaintext.$(i=1, 2)$
Let $v_i \in Fq$ be the random number. $(i=1, 2)$
$M_i \in O$ and $p_i \in Fq$ are defined as follows. $(i=1, 2)$

$$M_1 = u_1\mathbf{1} + v_1 B + w_1 H \bmod q \in O,$$

$$p_1 := u_1 + 2b_0 v_1 \bmod q,$$

$$M_2 = u_2\mathbf{1} + v_2 B + w_2 H \bmod q \in O,$$

$$p_2 := u_2 + 2b_0 v_2 \bmod q.$$

We calculate $E(M_1, E(M_2, X)) \bmod q$ by using (4.11) (see chapter 4) such that for any $A \bmod q \in O$

$$B(BA) = B^2 A \bmod q \in O,$$

$$H(HA) = H^2 A \bmod q \in O.$$

$E(M_1, E(M_2, X)) \bmod q$

$= A_1((\ldots((A_k((M_1(M_2[(A_k^{-1}((\ldots((A_1^{-1}X)Z_1))\ldots))Z_k])Z_k^{-1}))\ldots))Z_1^{-1}) \bmod q$

$= A_1((\ldots((A_k(([u_11+v_1B+w_1H][u_21+v_2B+w_2H]([(A_k^{-1}((\ldots((A_1^{-1}X)Z_1))\ldots))Z_k]) \quad Z_k^{-1}))\ldots))Z_1^{-1}) \bmod q$

$= A_1((\ldots((A_k(([u_11][u_21+v_2B+w_2H]([(A_k^{-1}((\ldots((A_1^{-1}X)Z_1))\ldots))Z_k]) Z_k^{-1}))\ldots))Z_1^{-1}) +$
$A_1((\ldots((A_k(([v_1B][u_21+v_2B+w_2H]([(A_k^{-1}((\ldots((A_1^{-1}X)Z_1))\ldots))Z_k]) Z_k^{-1}))\ldots))Z_1^{-1}) +$
$A_1((\ldots((A_k(([w_1H][u_21+v_2B+w_2H]([(A_k^{-1}((\ldots((A_1^{-1}X)Z_1))\ldots))Z_k])Z_k^{-1}))\ldots))Z_1^{-1})$
$\bmod q$

$= A_1((\ldots((A_k(([u_11][u_21]([(A_k^{-1}((\ldots((A_1^{-1}X)Z_1))\ldots))Z_k]) Z_k^{-1}))\ldots))Z_1^{-1}) +$
$A_1((\ldots((A_k(([u_11]([v_2B]([(A_k^{-1}((\ldots((A_1^{-1}X)Z_1))\ldots))Z_k]) Z_k^{-1}))\ldots))Z_1^{-1}) +$
$A_1((\ldots((A_k(([u_11]([w_2H]([(A_k^{-1}((\ldots((A_1^{-1}X)Z_1))\ldots))Z_k]) Z_k^{-1}))\ldots))Z_1^{-1}) +$
$A_1((\ldots((A_k(([v_1B][u_21]([(A_k^{-1}((\ldots((A_1^{-1}X)Z_1))\ldots))Z_k]) Z_k^{-1}))\ldots))Z_1^{-1}) +$
$A_1((\ldots((A_k(([v_1B]([v_2B]([(A_k^{-1}((\ldots((A_1^{-1}X)Z_1))\ldots))Z_k]) Z_k^{-1}))\ldots))Z_1^{-1}) +$
$A_1((\ldots((A_k(([v_1B]([w_2H]([(A_k^{-1}((\ldots((A_1^{-1}X)Z_1))\ldots))Z_k]) Z_k^{-1}))\ldots))Z_1^{-1}) +$
$A_1((\ldots((A_k(([w_1H][u_21]([(A_k^{-1}((\ldots((A_1^{-1}X)Z_1))\ldots))Z_k])Z_k^{-1}))\ldots))Z_1^{-1}) +$
$A_1((\ldots((A_k(([w_1H]([v_2B]([(A_k^{-1}((\ldots((A_1^{-1}X)Z_1))\ldots))Z_k])Z_k^{-1}))\ldots))Z_1^{-1}) +$
$A_1((\ldots((A_k(([w_1H]([w_2H]([(A_k^{-1}((\ldots((A_1^{-1}X)Z_1))\ldots))Z_k])Z_k^{-1}))\ldots))Z_1^{-1}) \bmod q$

$= A_1((\ldots((A_k(([u_11u_21+(v_1u_2+u_1v_2)B+v_1Bv_2B+(w_1u_2+u_1w_2)H+w_1Hw_2H][(A_k^{-1}((\ldots((A_1^{-1}X)Z_1))\ldots))Z_k]) Z_k^{-1}))\ldots))Z_1^{-1}) \bmod q$

$= A_1((\ldots((A_k(([(u_11+v_1B+w_2H)(u_21+v_2B+w_2H)][(A_k^{-1}((\ldots((A_1^{-1}X)Z_1))\ldots))Z_k])Z_k^{-1}))\ldots))Z_1^{-1}) \bmod q$

$= A_1((\ldots((A_k(([M_1M_2] [(A_k^{-1}((\ldots((A_1^{-1}X)Z_1))\ldots))Z_k])Z_k^{-1})) \ldots))Z_1^{-1}) \bmod q$

$= E(M_1M_2, X) \bmod q.$

We obtain p_1p_2 from M_1M_2 as follows.

$$M_1M_2 = (u_11+v_1B+w_2H)(u_21+v_2B+w_2H) \bmod q$$

$$= u_11u_21+(v_1u_2+u_1v_2)B+v_1Bv_2B+(w_1u_2+u_1w_2)H+w_1Hw_2H \bmod q$$

$$= u_1 u_2 \mathbf{1} + (v_1 u_2 + u_1 v_2 + 2 b_0 v_1 v_2) B + (w_1 u_2 + u_1 w_2 + 2 b_0 w_1 w_2) H \bmod q.$$

Let p_{12} be the plaintext of the ciphertext $E(M_1 M_2, X)$.

Then we have from difinition of plaintex

$$p_{12} = u_1 u_2 + 2 b_0 (v_1 u_2 + u_1 v_2 + 2 b_0 v_1 v_2) \bmod q$$

$$= (u_1 + 2 b_0 v_1)(u_2 + 2 b_0 v_2) \bmod q$$

$$= p_1 p_2 \bmod q.$$

In chapter 4 the fully homomorphic encryption scheme using the above property of examples is proposed.

CHAPTER 4

PROPOSED FULLY HOMOMORPHIC ENCRYPTION

SUMMARY: Gentry's bootstrapping technique is still the only known method for obtaining fully homomorphic encryption. I propose a new fully homomorphic encryption scheme on non-associative octonion ring over finite field without bootstrapping technique. The security of the proposed fully homomorphic encryption scheme is based on computational difficulty to solve the multivariate algebraic equations of high degree while the almost all multivariate cryptosystems [4.1],[4.2],[4.3] proposed until now are based on the quadratic equations avoiding the explosion of the coefficients. Because proposed fully homomorphic encryption scheme is based on multivariate algebraic equations with high degree or too many variables, it is against the Gröbner basis [1.1] attack, the differential attack, rank attack and so on.

The key size of this system and complexity for enciphering/deciphering become to be small enough to handle.

keywords: fully homomorphic encryption, multivariate algebraic equation, Gröbner basis, octonion

§1. Introduction

A cryptosystem which supports both addition and multiplication (thereby preserving the ring structure of the plaintexts) is known as fully homomorphic encryption (FHE) and is very powerful. Using such a scheme, any circuit can be homomorphically evaluated, effectively allowing the construction of programs which may be run on encryptions of their inputs to produce an encryption of their output. Since such a scheme does not decrypt its input, it can be run by an untrusted party without revealing its inputs and internal state. The existence of the cryptographical schemes with efficiency and fully homomorphism brings great practical implications in the outsourcing of private computations, for instance, in the context of cloud computing.

With homomorphic encryption, a company could encrypt its entire database of e-mails and upload it to a cloud. Then it could use the cloud-stored data as desired—for example, to calculate the stochastic value of stored data. The results would be downloaded and decrypted without ever exposing the details of a single e-mail.

In 2009 Gentry, an IBM researcher, has created a homomorphic encryption scheme that makes it possible to encrypt the data in such a way that performing a mathematical operation on the encrypted information and then decrypting the result produces the same answer as performing an analogous operation on the unencrypted data.

But in Gentry's scheme a task like finding a piece of text in an e-mail requires chaining together thousands of basic operations. His solution was to use a second layer of encryption, essentially to protect intermediate results when the system broke down and needed to be reset.

In this chapter I propose a fully homomorphic encryption scheme on non-associative octonion ring over finite field which is based on computational difficulty to solve the multivariate algebraic equations of high degree while the almost all multivariate cryptosystems [4.1],[4.2],[4.3] proposed until now are based on the quadratic equations avoiding the explosion of the coefficients. Our scheme is against the Gröbner basis [1.1] attack, the differential attack, rank attack and so on.

§2. Preliminaries for octonion operation

In this section we describe the operations on octonion ring and properties of octonion ring.

§2.1 Multiplication and addition on the octonion ring O

Let q be a fixed modulus to be as large prime as 2^{10}.
   Let O be the octonion [0.2] ring over a finite field Fq.

$$O=\{(a_0,a_1,...,a_7) \mid a_j \in Fq \ (j=0,1,...,7)\} \qquad (4.1)$$

We define the multiplication and addition of $A, B \in O$ as follows.

$$A=(a_0,a_1,...,a_7),\ a_j \in Fq \ (j=0,1,...,7), \qquad (4.2)$$

$$B=(b_0,b_1,...,b_7),\ b_j \in Fq \ (j=0,1,...,7). \qquad (4.3)$$

$AB \bmod q$

$$= (a_0b_0 - a_1b_1 - a_2b_2 - a_3b_3 - a_4b_4 - a_5b_5 - a_6b_6 - a_7b_7 \bmod q,$$

$$a_0b_1 + a_1b_0 + a_2b_4 + a_3b_7 - a_4b_2 + a_5b_6 - a_6b_5 - a_7b_3 \bmod q,$$

$$a_0b_2 - a_1b_4 + a_2b_0 + a_3b_5 + a_4b_1 - a_5b_3 + a_6b_7 - a_7b_6 \bmod q,$$

$$a_0b_3-a_1b_7-a_2b_5+a_3b_0+a_4b_6+a_5b_2-a_6b_4+a_7b_1 \text{ mod } q,$$

$$a_0b_4+a_1b_2-a_2b_1-a_3b_6+a_4b_0+a_5b_7+a_6b_3-a_7b_5 \text{ mod } q,$$

$$a_0b_5-a_1b_6+a_2b_3-a_3b_2-a_4b_7+a_5b_0+a_6b_1+a_7b_4 \text{ mod } q,$$

$$a_0b_6+a_1b_5-a_2b_7+a_3b_4-a_4b_3-a_5b_1+a_6b_0+a_7b_2 \text{ mod } q,$$

$$a_0b_7+a_1b_3+a_2b_6-a_3b_1+a_4b_5-a_5b_4-a_6b_2+a_7b_0 \text{ mod } q) \tag{4.4}$$

$A+B \text{ mod } q$

$$=(a_0+b_0 \text{ mod } q, \ a_1+b_1 \text{ mod } q, \ a_2+b_2 \text{ mod } q, \ a_3+b_3 \text{ mod } q,$$

$$a_4+b_4 \text{ mod } q, \ a_5+b_5 \text{ mod } q, \ a_6+b_6 \text{ mod } q, \ a_7+b_7 \text{ mod } q \ ). \tag{4.5}$$

Let

$$|A|^2= a_0^2+a_1^2+\ldots+a_7^2 \text{ mod } q. \tag{4.6}$$

If $|A|^2 \neq 0 \text{ mod } q$, we can have A^{-1}, the inverse of A by using the algorithm **Octinv**(A) such that

$$A^{-1}= (a_0/|A|^2 \text{ mod } q, \ -a_1/|A|^2 \text{ mod } q,\ldots, \ -a_7/|A|^2 \text{ mod } q) \ \leftarrow \ \textbf{Octinv}(A). \tag{4.7}$$

Here details of the algorithm **Octinv**(A) are omitted and can be looked up in the **Appendix A.**

§2.2 Order of the element in O

In this section we describe the order "J" of the element "A" in octonion ring, that is,

$$A^{J+1}=A \text{ mod } q.$$

Theorem 4.1.

Let $A:=(a_{10},a_{11},\ldots,a_{17}) \in O$, $a_{1j} \in Fq$ $(j=0,1,\ldots,7)$.

Let $(a_{n0},a_{n1},\ldots,a_{n7}) :=A^n \in O$, $a_{nj} \in Fq$ $(n=1,2,\ldots;j=0,1,\ldots,7)$.

a_{00}, a_{nj}'s$(n=1,2,\ldots;j=0,1,\ldots)$ and b_n's$(n=0,1,\ldots)$ satisfy the equations such that

$$N:= a_{11}^2+\ldots+a_{17}^2 \quad \text{mod } q$$

$$a_{00}:=1, \ b_0:=0, \ b_1:=1,$$

$$a_{n0}= a_{n-1,0}\,a_{10}-b_{n-1}N \text{ mod } q ,(n=1,2,\ldots), \tag{4.8}$$

$$b_n= a_{n-1,0}+b_{n-1}a_{10} \text{ mod } q ,(n=1,2,\ldots), \tag{4.9}$$

$$a_{nj} = b_n a_{1j} \bmod q \,, (n=1,2,\ldots;j=1,2,\ldots,7).$$ (4.10)

(*Proof:*)

Here proof is omitted and can be looked up in the **Appendix B**.

Theorem 4.2.

For an element $A=(a_{10}, a_{11}, \ldots, a_{17}) \in O$,

$$A^{J+1} = A \bmod q,$$

where

$$J = \text{LCM} \{q^2-1, q-1\} = q^2-1,$$

$$N := a_{11}^2 + a_{12}^2 + \ldots + a_{17}^2 \neq 0 \bmod q.$$

(*Proof:*)

Here proof is omitted and can be looked up in the **Appendix C**.

§2.3. Property of multiplication over octonion ring O

A, B, C etc. $\in O$ satisfy the following formulae in general where A, B and C have the inverse A^{-1}, B^{-1} and C^{-1} mod q.

1) Non-commutative

$$AB \neq BA \quad \bmod q.$$

2) Non-associative

$$A(BC) \neq (AB)C \quad \bmod q.$$

3) Alternative

$$(AA)B = A(AB) \quad \bmod q,$$ (4.11)

$$A(BB) = (AB)B \quad \bmod q,$$ (4.12)

$$(AB)A = A(BA) \quad \bmod q.$$ (4.13)

4) Moufang's formulae [0.2],

$$C(A(CB)) = ((CA)C)B \quad \bmod q,$$ (4.14)

$$A(C(BC)) = ((AC)B)C \quad \bmod q,$$ (4.15)

$$(CA)(BC)=(C(AB))C \quad \mod q, \tag{4.16}$$

$$(CA)(BC)=C((AB)C) \quad \mod q. \tag{4.17}$$

5) For positive integers n,m, we have

$$(AB)B^n =((AB)B^{n-1})B=A(B(B^{n-1}B))=AB^{n+1} \quad \mod q, \tag{4.18}$$

$$(AB^n)B =((AB)B^{n-1})B=A(B(B^{n-1}B))=AB^{n+1} \quad \mod q, \tag{4.19}$$

$$B^n (BA) =B(B^{n-1}(BA))= ((BB^{n-1})B)A=B^{n+1}A \quad \mod q, \tag{4.20}$$

$$B(B^n A)=B(B^{n-1}(BA))= ((BB^{n-1})B)A=B^{n+1}A \quad \mod q. \tag{4.21}$$

From (4.12) and (4.19), we have

$$[(AB^n)B]B =[AB^{n+1}]B \quad \mod q,$$

$$(AB^n)(BB) =[(AB^n)B]B =[AB^{n+1}]B= AB^{n+2} \quad \mod q,$$

$$(AB^n)B^2= AB^{n+2} \quad \mod q,$$

$$\cdots \qquad \cdots$$

$$(AB^n)B^m= AB^{n+m} \quad \mod q.$$

In the same way we have

$$B^m(B^n A)= B^{n+m}A \quad \mod q.$$

6) **Lemma 4.1.**

$$A(B((AB)^n))=(AB)^{n+1} \quad \mod q,$$

$$(((AB)^n)A)B =(AB)^{n+1} \quad \mod q.$$

where n is a positive integer and B has the inverse B^{-1}.

(*Proof.*)

From (4.14) we have

$$B(A(B((AB)^n)=((BA)B)(AB)^n=(B(AB))(AB)^n=B(AB)^{n+1} \quad \mod q.$$

Then

$$B^{-1}(B(A(B(AB)^n))= B^{-1}(B (AB)^{n+1}) \quad \mod q,$$

$$A(B(AB)^n)= (AB)^{n+1} \quad \mod q.$$

In the same way we have

$$(((AB)^n)A)B=(AB)^{n+1} \mod q. \qquad \text{q.e.d.}$$

7) **Lemma 4.2.**

$$A^{-1}(AB)= B \mod q,$$

$$(BA)A^{-1}= B \mod q.$$

(*Proof:*)

Here proof is omitted and can be looked up in the **Appendix D**.

8) **Lemma 4.3.**

$$A(BA^{-1})= (AB)A^{-1} \mod q.$$

(*Proof:*)

From (4.17) we substitute A^{-1} to C, we have

$$(A^{-1}A)(B\,A^{-1})= A^{-1}((AB)\,A^{-1}) \mod q,$$

$$(B\,A^{-1})= A^{-1}((AB)\,A^{-1}) \mod q.$$

We multiply A from left side,

$$A(B\,A^{-1})= A(A^{-1}((AB)\,A^{-1}))= (AB)\,A^{-1} \mod q. \qquad \text{q.e.d.}$$

We can express $A(BA^{-1})$, $(AB)A^{-1}$ such that

$$ABA^{-1}.$$

9) From (4.13) and Lemma 4.2 we have

$$A^{-1}((A(BA^{-1}))A)= A^{-1}(A((BA^{-1})A))= (BA^{-1})A=B \mod q,$$

$$(A^{-1}((AB)A^{-1}))A=((A^{-1}(AB))A^{-1})A= A^{-1}(AB)=B \mod q.$$

10) **Lemma 4.4.**

$$(BA^{-1})(AB)=B^2 \mod q.$$

(*Proof:*)

From (4.17),

$$(BA^{-1})(AB)=B((A^{-1}A)B)=B^2 \mod q. \qquad \text{q.e.d.}$$

11) Lemma 4.5a

$$(ABA^{-1})(ABA^{-1}) = AB^2A^{-1} \bmod q.$$

(*Proof:*)

From (4.17),

$$(ABA^{-1})(ABA^{-1}) \quad \bmod q$$

$$= [A^{-1}(A^2(BA^{-1}))][(AB)A^{-1}] = A^{-1}\{[(A^2(BA^{-1}))(AB)]A^{-1}\} \quad \bmod q$$

$$= A^{-1}\{[(A(A(BA^{-1})))(AB)]A^{-1}\} \quad \bmod q$$

$$= A^{-1}\{[(A((AB)A^{-1}))(AB)]A^{-1}\} \quad \bmod q$$

$$= A^{-1}\{[(A(AB))A^{-1}))(AB)]A^{-1}\} \quad \bmod q.$$

We apply (4.15) to inside of [.],

$$= A^{-1}\{[(A((AB)(A^{-1}(AB))))]A^{-1}\} \quad \bmod q$$

$$= A^{-1}\{[(A((AB)B))]A^{-1}\} \quad \bmod q$$

$$= A^{-1}\{[A(A(BB))]A^{-1}\} \quad \bmod q$$

$$= \{A^{-1}[A(A(BB))]\}A^{-1} \quad \bmod q$$

$$= (A(BB))A^{-1} \quad \bmod q$$

$$= AB^2A^{-1} \bmod q. \qquad\qquad \text{q.e.d.}$$

11b) Lemma 5b

$$[A_1(\ldots(A_rBA_r^{-1})\ldots)A_1^{-1}]\,[A_1(\ldots(A_rBA_r^{-1})\ldots)A_1^{-1}]$$

$$= A_1(\ldots(A_rB^2A_r^{-1})\ldots)A_1^{-1} \bmod q.$$

where

$$A_i \in O \text{ has the inverse } A_i^{-1} \bmod q \ (i=1,\ldots,r).$$

(*Proof:*)

As we use Lemma 5a repeatedly we have

$$\{A_1([A_2(\ldots(A_rBA_r^{-1})\ldots)A_2^{-1}])A_1^{-1}\}\{A_1([A_2(\ldots(A_rBA_r^{-1})\ldots)A_2^{-1}])A_1^{-1}\} \bmod q$$

$$= A_1([A_2(\ldots(A_rBA_r^{-1})\ldots)A_2^{-1}][A_2(\ldots(A_rBA_r^{-1})\ldots)A_2^{-1}])A_1^{-1} \bmod q$$

$$= A_1(A_2([A_3(\ldots(A_rBA_r^{-1})\ldots)A_3^{-1}][A_3(\ldots(A_rBA_r^{-1})\ldots)A_3^{-1}]A_2^{-1}])A_1^{-1} \bmod q$$

$$\cdots \qquad\qquad \cdots$$

$$= A_1(A_2(\ldots([A_rBA_r^{-1}]\,[A_rBA_r^{-1}])\ldots)A_2^{-1})A_1^{-1} \bmod q$$

$$= A_1(A_2(\ldots(A_rB^2A_r^{-1})\ldots)A_2^{-1})A_1^{-1} \bmod q$$

q.e.d.

11c) **Lemma 5c**

$$A_1^{-1}\,(A_1BA_1^{-1})\,A_1$$

$$= B \bmod q.$$

where

$$A_1 \in O \text{ has the inverse } A_1^{-1} \bmod q.$$

(*Proof*:)

$$A_1^{-1}\,(A_1BA_1^{-1})\,A_1 = A_1^{-1}\,[((A_1B)A_1^{-1})\,A_1] \bmod q,$$

from Lemma 2 we have

$$= A_1^{-1}\,(A_1B) = B \bmod q. \qquad \text{q.e.d.}$$

11d) **Lemma 5d**

$$A_r^{-1}\,(\ldots(A_1^{-1}\,[A_1(\ldots(A_rBA_r^{-1})\ldots)A_1^{-1}]\,A_1)\ldots)A_r$$

$$= B \bmod q.$$

where

$$A_i \in O \text{ has the inverse } A_i^{-1}\bmod q\ (i=1,\ldots,r).$$

(*Proof*:)

As we use Lemma 5c repeatedly we have

$$A_r^{-1}\,(\ldots(A_1^{-1}\,[A_1(\ldots(A_rBA_r^{-1})\ldots)A_1^{-1}]\,A_1)\ldots)A_r$$

$$= A_r^{-1}\,(\ldots(A_2^{-1}\,[A_2(\ldots(A_rBA_r^{-1})\ldots)A_2^{-1}]\,A_2)\ldots)A_r \bmod q$$

$$\cdots \qquad\qquad \cdots$$

$$= A_r^{-1}[A_rBA_r^{-1}]A_r \bmod q$$

$$= B \bmod q \qquad \text{q.e.d.}$$

12) **Lemma 4.6.**

$$(AB^m A^{-1})(AB^n A^{-1}) = AB^{m+n} A^{-1} \quad \mod q.$$

(*Proof:*)

From (4.16),

$$[A^{-1}(A^2(B^m A^{-1}))][(AB^n)A^{-1}] = \{A^{-1}[(A^2(B^m A^{-1}))(AB^n)]\}A^{-1} \quad \mod q$$

$$= A^{-1}\{[(A(A(B^m A^{-1}))(AB^n)]A^{-1}\} \quad \mod q$$

$$= A^{-1}\{[(A((AB^m)A^{-1}))(AB^n)]A^{-1}\} \quad \mod q$$

$$= A^{-1}\{[((A(AB^m))A^{-1}))(AB^n)]A^{-1}\} \quad \mod q$$

$$= A^{-1}\{[((A^2 B^m)A^{-1}))(AB^n)]A^{-1}\} \quad \mod q.$$

We apply (4.15) to inside of { . },

$$= A^{-1}\{(A^2 B^m)[A^{-1}((AB^n)A^{-1})]\} \quad \mod q$$

$$= A^{-1}\{(A^2 B^m)[A^{-1}(A(B^n A^{-1}))]\} \quad \mod q$$

$$= A^{-1}\{(A^2 B^m)(B^n A^{-1})\} \quad \mod q$$

$$= A^{-1}\{(A^{-1}(A^3 B^m))(B^n A^{-1})\} \quad \mod q.$$

We apply (4.17) to inside of { . },

$$= A^{-1}\{A^{-1}([(A^3 B^m)B^n]A^{-1})]\} \quad \mod q$$

$$= A^{-1}\{A^{-1}((A^3 B^{m+n})A^{-1})\} \quad \mod q$$

$$= A^{-1}\{(A^{-1}(A^3 B^{m+n}))A^{-1}\} \quad \mod q$$

$$= A^{-1}\{(A^2 B^{m+n})A^{-1}\} \quad \mod q$$

$$= \{A^{-1}(A^2 B^{m+n}))\}A^{-1} \quad \mod q$$

$$= (AB^{m+n})A^{-1} \quad \mod q$$

$$= AB^{m+n} A^{-1} \mod q. \qquad\qquad \text{q.e.d}$$

13) $A \in O$ satisfies the following theorem.

Theorem 4.3.

$$A^2 = w\mathbf{1} + vA \mod q,$$

where

$$^{\exists}w,v \in Fq,$$

$$\mathbf{1}=(1,0,0,0,0,0,0,0) \in O,$$

$$A=(a_0,a_1,\ldots,a_7) \in O.$$

(*Proof:*)

$A^2 \bmod q$

$=(\quad a_0a_0-a_1a_1-a_2a_2-a_3a_3-a_4a_4-a_5a_5-a_6a_6-a_7a_7 \bmod q,$

$\quad a_0a_1+a_1a_0+a_2a_4+a_3a_7-a_4a_2+a_5a_6-a_6a_5-a_7a_3 \bmod q,$

$\quad a_0a_2-a_1a_4+a_2a_0+a_3a_5+a_4a_1-a_5a_3+a_6a_7-a_7a_6 \bmod q,$

$\quad a_0a_3-a_1a_7-a_2a_5+a_3a_0+a_4a_6+a_5a_2-a_6a_4+a_7a_1 \bmod q,$

$\quad a_0a_4+a_1a_2-a_2a_1-a_3a_6+a_4a_0+a_5a_7+a_6a_3-a_7a_5 \bmod q,$

$\quad a_0a_5-a_1a_6+a_2a_3-a_3a_2-a_4a_7+a_5a_0+a_6a_1+a_7a_4 \bmod q,$

$\quad a_0a_6+a_1a_5-a_2a_7+a_3a_4-a_4a_3-a_5a_1+a_6a_0+a_7a_2 \bmod q,$

$\quad a_0a_7+a_1a_3+a_2a_6-a_3a_1+a_4a_5-a_5a_4-a_6a_2+a_7a_0 \bmod q)$

$=(2a_0^2- L \bmod q, 2a_0a_1 \bmod q, 2a_0a_2 \bmod q, 2a_0a_3 \bmod q, 2a_0a_4 \bmod q, 2a_0a_5 \bmod q,$

$$2a_0a_6 \bmod q, 2a_0a_7 \bmod q)$$

where

$$L= a_0^2+a_1^2+a_2^2+a_3^2+a_4^2+a_5^2+a_6^2+a_7^2 \bmod q.$$

Now we try to obtain $u,\ v \in Fq$ that satisfy $A^2=w\mathbf{1}+vA \bmod q$.

$$w\mathbf{1}+vA= w(1,0,0,0,0,0,0,0)+v(a_0,a_1,\ldots,a_7) \bmod q,$$

$A^2= (2a_0^2- L \bmod q, 2a_0a_1 \bmod q, 2a_0a_2 \bmod q, 2a_0a_3 \bmod q, 2a_0a_4 \bmod q,$

$$2a_0a_5 \bmod q, 2a_0a_6 \bmod q, 2a_0a_7 \bmod q).$$

Then we have

$$A^2=w\mathbf{1}+vA=-L\mathbf{1}+2 a_0A \bmod q,$$

$$w= -L \bmod q,$$

$$v=2a_0 \bmod q. \qquad\qquad \text{q.e.d.}$$

14) **Theorem 4.4.**

$$A^h = w_h\mathbf{1} + v_hA \bmod q$$

where h is an integer and $w_h, v_h \in Fq$.

(*Proof:*)

From Theorem 4.3

$$A^2 = w_2\mathbf{1} + v_2A = -L\mathbf{1} + 2a_0A \bmod q.$$

If we can express A^h such that

$$A^h = w_h\mathbf{1} + v_hA \bmod q \in O, \; w_h, v_h \in Fq,$$

Then

$$A^{h+1} = (w_h\mathbf{1} + v_hA)A \bmod q$$

$$= w_hA + v_h(-L\mathbf{1} + 2\,a_0A) \bmod q$$

$$= -Lv_h\mathbf{1} + (w_h + 2a_0v_h)A \bmod q.$$

We have

$$w_{h+1} = -Lv_h \bmod q \in Fq,$$

$$v_{h+1} = w_h + 2a_0v_h \bmod q \in Fq. \qquad \text{q.e.d.}$$

15) **Theorem 4.5.**

$D \in O$ does not exist that satisfies the following equation.

$$B(AX) = DX \bmod q,$$

where $B, A, D \in O$, and X is a variable.

(*Proof:*)

When $X = \mathbf{1}$, we have

$$BA = D \bmod q.$$

Then

$$B(AX) = (BA)X \bmod q.$$

We can select $C \in O$ that satisfies

$$B(AC) \neq (BA)C \bmod q \qquad (4.22)$$

We substitute $C \in O$ to X to obtain

$$B(AC)=(BA)C. \bmod q \tag{4.23}$$

(4.23) is contradictory to (4.22).   q.e.d.

16) **Theorem 4.6.**

$D \in O$ does not exist that satisfies the following equation.

$$C(B(AX))=DX \bmod q \tag{4.24}$$

where $C,B,A,D \in O$, C has inverse $C^{-1} \bmod q$ and X is a variable.

    B,A,C are non-associative, that is,

$$B(AC) \neq (BA)C \bmod q. \tag{4.25}$$

(*Proof*:)

If D exists, we have at $X=1$

$$C(BA)=D \bmod q.$$

Then

$$C(B(AX))=(C(BA))X \bmod q.$$

We substitute C to X to obtain

$$C(B(AC))=(C(BA))C \bmod q.$$

From (4.13)

$$C(B(AC))=(C(BA))C=C((BA)C) \bmod q$$

Multiplying C^{-1} from left side ,

$$B(AC)=(BA)C \bmod q \tag{4.26}$$

(4.26) is contradictory to (4.25).   q.e.d.

17) **Theorem 4.7**

D and $E \in O$ do not exist that satisfy the following equation.

$$C(B(AX))= E\,(DX) \bmod q$$

where C,B,A,D and $E \in O$ have inverse and X is a variable.

A,B,C are non-associative, that is,

$$C(BA) \neq (CB)A \bmod q. \tag{4.27}$$

(*Proof:*)

If D and E exist, we have at $X=1$

$$C(BA)=ED \bmod \tag{4.28}$$

We have at $X=(ED)^{-1}=D^{-1}E^{-1} \bmod q$.

$$C(B(A(D^{-1}E^{-1})))= E \, (D(D^{-1}E^{-1})) \bmod q=1$$

$$(C(B(A(D^{-1}E^{-1})))^{-1} \bmod q=1$$

$$((ED)A^{-1})B^{-1})C^{-1} \bmod q=1$$

$$ED =(CB)A \bmod. \tag{4.29}$$

From (4.28) and (4.29) we have

$$C(BA) =(CB)A \bmod \tag{4.30}$$

(4.30) is contradictory to (4.27).   q.e.d.

18) **Theorem 4.8.**

$D \in O$ does not exist that satisfies the following equation.

$$A(B(A^{-1}X))=DX \bmod q$$

where $B,A,D \in O$, A has inverse $A^{-1} \bmod q$ and X is a variable.

(*Proof:*)

If D exists, we have at $X=1$

$$A(BA^{-1})=D \bmod q.$$

Then

$$A\,(B(A^{-1}X))=(A(BA^{-1}))X \bmod q \tag{4.31}$$

We can select $C \in O$ such that

$$(BA^{-1})(CA^2) \neq (BA^{-1})C)A^2 \bmod q. \tag{4.32}$$

That is, (BA^{-1}), C and A^2 are non-associative.

Substituing $X=CA$ in (4.31), we have

$$A(B(A^{-1}(CA)))=(A(BA^{-1}))(CA) \bmod q,$$

from Lemma 4.3.

$$A(B((A^{-1}C)A)))=(A(BA^{-1}))(CA) \bmod q,$$

from (4.17)

$$A(B((A^{-1}C)A)))=A([(BA^{-1})C]A) \bmod q.$$

Multiply A^{-1} from left side we have

$$B((A^{-1}C)A))=((BA^{-1})C)A \bmod q,$$

from Lemma 4.3.

$$B(A^{-1}(CA))=((BA^{-1})C)A \bmod q.$$

Transforming CA to $((CA^2)A^{-1})$, we have

$$B(A^{-1}((CA^2)A^{-1}))=((BA^{-1})C)A \bmod q.$$

From (4.15) we have

$$((BA^{-1})(CA^2))A^{-1}=((BA^{-1})C)A \bmod q.$$

Multiply A from right side we have

$$((BA^{-1})(CA^2)=((BA^{-1})C)A^2 \bmod q. \tag{4.33}$$

(4.33) is contradictory to (4.32). q.e.d.

§3. Concept of proposed fully homomorphic encryption scheme

Homomorphic encryption is a form of encryption which allows specific types of computations to be carried out on ciphertext and obtain an encrypted result which decrypted matches the result of operations performed on the plaintext. For instance, one person could add two encrypted numbers and then another person could decrypt the result, without either of them being able to find the value of the individual numbers.

§3.1 Definition of homomorphic encryption

A homomorphic encryption scheme **HE** := (**KeyGen; Enc; Dec; Eval**) is a quadruple of PPT (Probabilistic polynomial time) algorithms.

In this work, the medium text space M_e of the encryption schemes will be octonion ring, and the functions to be evaluated will be represented as arithmetic circuits over this ring, composed of addition and multiplication gates. The syntax of these algorithms is given as follows.

-Key-Generation. The algorithm **KeyGen**, on input the security parameter 1^λ, outputs $(\mathbf{sk}) \leftarrow \mathbf{KeyGen}(1^\lambda)$, where **sk** is a secret encryption/decryption key.

-Encryption. The algorithm **Enc**, on input system parameter q, secret keys(**sk**) and a plaintext $p \in Fq$, outputs a ciphertext $C \leftarrow \mathbf{Enc}(\mathbf{sk}; p)$.

-Decryption. The algorithm **Dec**, on input system parameter q, secret key(**sk**) and a ciphertext C, outputs a plaintext $p^* \leftarrow \mathbf{Dec}(\mathbf{sk}; C)$.

-Homomorphic-Evaluation. The algorithm **Eval**, on input system parameter q, an arithmetic circuit ckt, and a tuple of n ciphertexts $(C_1, \ldots, C_n)$, outputs a ciphertext $C' \leftarrow \mathbf{Eval}(\text{ckt}; C_1, \ldots, C_n)$.

The security notion needed in this scheme is security against chosen plaintext attacks (**IND-CPA** security), defined as follows.

Definition (**IND-CPA security**). A scheme HE is **IND-CPA** secure if for any PPT adversary A_d it holds that:

$$\text{Adv}^{CPA}_{HE}[\lambda] := |\Pr[A_d(\mathbf{Enc}(\mathbf{sk}; 0)) = 1] - \Pr[A_d(\mathbf{Enc}(\mathbf{sk}; 1)) = 1]| = \text{negl}(\lambda)$$

where $(\mathbf{sk}) \leftarrow \mathbf{KeyGen}(1^\lambda)$.

§3.2 Definition of fully homomorphic encryption

A scheme HE is fully homomorphic if it is both compact and homomorphic with respect to a class of circuits. More formally:

Definition (**Fully homomorphic encryption**). A homomorphic encryption scheme FHE $:=$(**KeyGen; Enc; Dec; Eval**) is fully homomorphic if it satisfies the following properties:

1. Homomorphism: Let $CR = \{CR_\lambda\}_{\lambda \in N}$ be the set of all polynomial sized arithmetic circuits. On input **sk** $\leftarrow$**KeyGen**(1^λ), $\forall$ ckt $\in CR_\lambda$, $\forall (p_1,\ldots,p_n) \in Fq^n$ where $n = n(\lambda)$, $\forall (C_1,\ldots,C_n)$

where $C_i \leftarrow$ **Enc(sk**;p_i), it holds that:

$$\Pr[\textbf{Dec(sk;Eval}(\text{ckt}; C_1,\ldots,C_n)) \neq \text{ckt}(p_1,\ldots,p_n)] = \text{negl}(\lambda).$$

2. Compactness: There exists a polynomial $\mu = \mu(\lambda)$ such that the output length of **Eval** is at most μ bits long regardless of the input circuit ckt and the number of its inputs.

§3.3 Proposed fully homomorphic enciphering/deciphering functions

We propose a fully homomorphic encryption (FHE) scheme based on the enciphering/deciphering functions on octonion ring over Fq.

First we define the medium text M as follows.
We select the element $B=(b_0,b_1,b_2,\ldots,b_7)$ and $H=(b_0,-b_1,-b_2,\ldots,-b_7) \in O$ such that,

$$L_B:=|B|^2 = b_0^2+b_1^2+\ldots+b_7^2 \bmod q=0 \in Fq,$$

$$b_0 \neq 0 \bmod q \in Fq,$$

$$b_1 \neq 0 \bmod q \in Fq.$$

Then we have

$$L_H:=|H|^2 = b_0^2+b_1^2+\ldots+b_7^2 \bmod q=0 \in Fq,$$

$$B+H=2b_0\mathbf{1} \bmod q,$$

$$B^2=2b_0B \bmod q,$$

$$H^2=2b_0H \bmod q,$$

$$BH=HB=\mathbf{0} \bmod q.$$

Let $u,v \in Fq$ be sub-plaintexts where a plaintext p is given such as

$$p:=u+2b_0v \bmod q.$$

Let $w \in \mathbf{F}q$ be a random number.

We define the medium text M by

$$M := R_1(\ldots(R_r(u\mathbf{1}+vB+wH)R_r^{-1})\ldots)R_1^{-1} \in O,$$

where

$$p = u+2b_0v \bmod q,$$

$R_i \in O$ is selected such that $R_i^{-1} \in O$ exists ($i=1,\ldots,r$) and

$$R_iB \neq BR_i \bmod q(i=1,\ldots,r),$$

$$R_iH \neq H_i \bmod q(i=1,\ldots,r).$$

Then

$$|M|^2 = |R_1(\ldots(R_r(u\mathbf{1}+vB+wH)R_r^{-1})\ldots)R_1^{-1}|^2$$

$$= (u+b_0(v+w))^2+(v-w)^2(b_0^2+b_1^2+\ldots+b_7^2) \bmod q,$$

$$= (u+b_0(v+w))^2-(v-w)^2b_0^2 \bmod q,$$

$$= (u+2b_0v)(u+2b_0w) \bmod q.$$

Here we simplify the expression of medium text M such that

$$M := \mathbf{R}(u+vB+wH)\mathbf{R}^{-1} \in O.$$

Let

$$M_1 := \mathbf{R}(u_1+v_1B+w_1H)\mathbf{R}^{-1} \in O,$$

$$p_1 = u_1+2b_0v_1 \bmod q,$$

$$M_2 := \mathbf{R}(u_2+v_2B+w_2H)\mathbf{R}^{-1} \in O,$$

$$p_2 = u_2+2b_0v_2 \bmod q.$$

We have

$$M_1M_2 = [\mathbf{R}(u_1\mathbf{1}+v_1B+w_1H)\mathbf{R}^{-1}][\mathbf{R}(u_2\mathbf{1}+v_2B+w_2H)\mathbf{R}^{-1}]$$

$$= \mathbf{R}[u_1u_2+(u_1v_2+v_1u_2+2b_0v_1v_2)B+(u_1w_2+w_1u_2+2b_0w_1w_2)H]\mathbf{R}^{-1}$$

$$= M_2M_1 \bmod q.$$

We show the reason as follows by using Lemma 5b.

$[R\ BR^{-1}][RBR^{-1}] = RB^2R^{-1} = 2\ b_0RBR^{-1} \bmod q,$

$[R\ HR^{-1}][RHR^{-1}] = RH^2R^{-1} = 2\ b_0RHR^{-1} \bmod q,$

and

$[R\ (B+H)R^{-1}] = [R\ B\ R^{-1} + R\ HR^{-1}] = 2\ b_0\mathbf{1} \bmod q.$

We multiply $[R\ BR^{-1}]$ from right side, we have

$[R\ B\ R^{-1} + R\ HR^{-1}]\ [R\ BR^{-1}] = 2\ b_0\mathbf{1}[R\ BR^{-1}] = 2\ b_0\ [R\ BR^{-1}] \bmod q,$

$2\ b_0\ [R\ B\ R^{-1}] + [R\ HR^{-1}]\ [R\ BR^{-1}] = 2\ b_0\ [R\ BR^{-1}] \bmod q.$

Then

$[R\ HR^{-1}][RBR^{-1}] = \mathbf{0} \bmod q.$

In the same manner we have

$[R\ BR^{-1}][RHR^{-1}] = \mathbf{0} \bmod q.$

Here I define the some parameters for describing FHE.

Let q be as a large prime such as $O(q) = 2^{80}$.

Let $M=(m_0,m_1,\ldots,m_7) = R(u\mathbf{1}+vB+wH)R^{-1} \in O$ be the medium plaintext.

Let $p := (u\mathbf{1}+2b_0v) \bmod q$.

Let $X=(x_0,\ldots,x_7) \in O[X]$ be a variable.

Let $E(p,X)$ and $D(X)$ be a enciphering and a deciphering function of user A.

Let $C(X)=E(p,X) \in O[X]$ be the ciphertext.

A_i, $Z_i \in O$ is selected randomly such that A_i^{-1} and Z_i^{-1} exist $(i=1,\ldots,k)$ which are the secret keys of user A.

Enciphering function $C(X)=E(p,X)$ is defined as follows.

$C(X)=E(p,X):=$

$$A_1((\ldots((A_k((M[(A_k^{-1}((\ldots((A_1^{-1}X)Z_1))\ldots))Z_k])Z_k^{-1}))\ldots))Z_1^{-1}) \bmod q \in O[X] \qquad (4.34)$$

$$= (\ e_{00}x_0+e_{01}x_1+\ldots+e_{07}x_7,$$

$$e_{10}x_0+e_{11}x_1+\ldots+e_{17}\,x_7,$$

$$\ldots \qquad \ldots$$

$$e_{70}x_0+e_{71}x_1+\ldots+e_{77}\,x_7), \qquad (4.35)$$

$$= \{e_{ij}\}(i,j=0,\ldots,7) \qquad (4.36)$$

with $e_{ij} \in Fq$ $(i,j=0,\ldots,7)$ which is published in cloud centre.

Here we notice how to construct enciphering function.

We show a part of process for constructing enciphering function $E(p,X)$ as follows.

$$A_1^{-1}X$$
$$(A_1^{-1}X)Z_1$$
$$A_2^{-1}((A_1^{-1}X)Z_1)$$
$$(A_2^{-1}((A_1^{-1}X)Z_1))\,Z_2$$
$$\ldots$$
$$(A_k^{-1}((\ldots((A_1^{-1}X)Z_1))\ldots))Z_k$$
$$M[(A_k^{-1}((\ldots((A_1^{-1}X)Z_1))\ldots))Z_k]$$
$$(M[(A_k^{-1}((\ldots((A_1^{-1}X)Z_1))\ldots))Z_k])Z_k^{-1}$$
$$A_k(M[(A_k^{-1}((\ldots((A_1^{-1}X)Z_1))\ldots))Z_k])Z_k^{-1})$$
$$\ldots$$
$$A_1((\ldots((A_k((M[(A_k^{-1}((\ldots((A_1^{-1}X)Z_1))\ldots))Z_k])Z_k^{-1}))\ldots))\,Z_1^{-1})$$

Let D be the deciphering function defined as follows .

$$G_1(X):=(A_k^{-1}((\ldots((A_1^{-1}X)Z_1))\ldots))Z_k, \tag{4.37}$$

$$G_2(X):=A_1((\ldots((A_k(X\,Z_k^{-1}))\ldots))\,Z_1^{-1}), \tag{4.38}$$

$$D(X):= G_1(C(G_2(X))\bmod q=MX. \tag{4.39}$$

$D(1)=M=(m_0,m_1,\ldots,m_7)=R_1(\ldots(R_r(u\mathbf{1}+vB+wH)\,R_r^{-1})\ldots)R_1^{-1}\in O$

$=R[u\mathbf{1}+vB+wH]R^{-1}\in O$

$= R[\,u\mathbf{1}+v(b_0,b_1,\ldots,b_7)+w(b_0,-b_1,\ldots,-b_7)\,]R^{-1}\in O.$

Then we obtain the plaintext p as follows.

Let $M'= u\mathbf{1}+vB+wH=(m_0', m_1',\ldots,m_7')=R'^{-1}(m_0,m_1,\ldots,m_7)\,R'\bmod q$

$:= R_r^{-1}(\ldots(R_1^{-1}(m_0,m_1,\ldots,m_7)\,R_1)\ldots)R_r\bmod q\in O.$

By solving the following equations, we have the plaintext p.

$$M'= u\mathbf{1}+vB+wH\bmod q\in O.$$

By multiplying B from rightside we have

$$M'B=(u+2b_0v)B\bmod q\in O.$$

Then we obtain p such that

$$p= u +2b_0v = [M'B]_0/b_0\ \bmod q\in Fq,$$

where we denote the first element of octonion M such as

$$[M]_0.$$

§3.4 Elements on octonion ring assumption EOR($k,r,n;q$)

Here we describe the assumption on which the proposed scheme bases.
Elements on octonion ring assumption EOR($k,r,n;q$).

Let q be a prime more than 2. Let k , r and n be integer parameters. Let
$A:=(A_1,\ldots,A_k) \in O^k$, $Z:=(Z_1,\ldots,Z_k) \in O^k$, $R:=(R_1,\ldots,R_r) \in O^r$. Let $C_i(X) := E(p_i ,X)=$
$(A_1((\ldots((A_k(M_i [(A_k^{-1}((\ldots((A_1^{-1}X)Z_1))\ldots))Z_k]))Z_k^{-1}))\ldots)) Z_1^{-1} \bmod q \in O[X]$ where
medium text $M_i=(m_{i0},\ldots, m_{i7}):= R_1(\ldots(R_r(u_i\mathbf{1}+v_iB+w_iH)R_r^{-1})\ldots)R_1^{-1} \in O$, plaintext $p_i =$
$u_i+2[B]_0v_i \bmod q (i=1,\ldots,n)$, X is a variable.

In the **EOR($k,r,n;q$)** assumption, the adversary A_d is given $C_i(X) (i=1,\ldots,n$)
randomly and his goal is to find a set of elements $A=(A_1,\ldots,A_k) \in O^k$, $Z=(Z_1,\ldots,Z_k) \in$
O^k, $R=(R_1,\ldots,R_r) \in O^r$, with the order of the elements $A_1,\ldots, A_k, Z_1,\ldots,Z_k, R_1,\ldots,R_r$
and plaintexts $p_i(i=1,\ldots,n)$. For parameters $k = k(\lambda)$, $r = r(\lambda)$ and $n=n(\lambda)$ defined in
terms of the security parameter λ and for any PPT adversary A_d we have

$\Pr [(A_1((\ldots((A_k(M_i[(A_k^{-1}((\ldots((A_1^{-1}X)Z_1))\ldots))Z_k]))Z_k^{-1}))\ldots)) Z_1^{-1} \bmod q = C_i(X)$
$(i=1,\ldots,n) : A=(A_1,\ldots, A_k), M_i(i=1,\ldots,n) \leftarrow A_d (1^\lambda, C_i(X) (i=1,\ldots,n))]= \mathrm{negl}(\lambda).$

To solve directly **EOR($k,r,n;q$)** assumption is known to be the problem for
solving the multivariate algebraic equations of high degree which is known to be NP-
hard.

§3.5 Syntax of proposed algorithms

The syntax of proposed scheme is given as follows.

-Key-Generation. The algorithm **KeyGen**, on input the security parameter 1^λ and
system parameter q, outputs $\mathbf{sk}=(A,Z,R,B,H) \leftarrow \mathbf{KeyGen}(1^\lambda)$, where $\mathbf{sk}$ is a secret
encryption /dencryption key.

-Encryption. The algorithm **Enc**, on input system parameter q, and secret keys
$\mathbf{sk}=(A,Z,R,B,H)$ and a plaintext $p \in Fq$, outputs a ciphertext
$C(X;\mathbf{sk},p) \leftarrow \mathbf{Enc}(\mathbf{sk};p)$.

-Decryption. The algorithm **Dec**, on input system parameter q, secret keys $\mathbf{sk}$ and
a ciphertext $C(X;\mathbf{sk},p)$, outputs plaintext $\mathbf{Dec}(\mathbf{sk}; C(X;\mathbf{sk},p))$ where $C(X;\mathbf{sk},p)$
$\leftarrow \mathbf{Enc}(\mathbf{sk}; p)$.

-Homomorphic-Evaluation. The algorithm **Eval**, on input system parameter q, an arithmetic circuit ckt, and a tuple of n ciphertexts $(C_1, \ldots, C_n)$, outputs an evaluated ciphertext $C' \leftarrow \mathbf{Eval}(\text{ckt}; C_1, \ldots, C_n)$ where $C_i = C(X; \mathbf{sk}, p_i)$ $(i=1, \ldots, n)$.

Theorem 9

For any $p, p' \in O$,

$$\text{if } E(p, X) = E(p', X) \bmod q \text{, then } p = p' \bmod q.$$

That is, if $p \neq p' \bmod q$, then $E(p, X) \neq E(p', X) \bmod q$.

(*Proof*)

If $E E(p, X) = E(p', X) \bmod q$, then

$$G_1(E(p, (G_2(X)) = G_1(E(p', (G_2(X)) \bmod q$$

$$MX = M'X \bmod q$$

where

$$M = R_1(\ldots(R_r((u\mathbf{1} + vB + wH)R_r^{-1})\ldots)R_1^{-1} \bmod q,$$

$$p = u + 2b_0v \bmod q,$$

$$M' = R_1(\ldots(R_r(u'\mathbf{1} + v'B + w'H)R_r^{-1})\ldots)R_1^{-1} \bmod q,$$

$$p' = u' + 2b_0v' \bmod q.$$

We substitute $\mathbf{1}$ to X in above expression, we obtain

$$M = M' \bmod q.$$

$$R_1(\ldots(R_r(u\mathbf{1} + vB + wH)R_r^{-1})\ldots)R_1^{-1}$$

$$= R_1(\ldots(R_r(u'\mathbf{1} + v'B + w'H)R_r^{-1})\ldots)R_1^{-1} \bmod q$$

$$u\mathbf{1} + vB + wH = u'\mathbf{1} + v'B + w'H \bmod q.$$

Then by multiplying B from rightside we have

$$uB + vB^2 + w HB = u'B + v'B^2 + w'HB \bmod q,$$

$$uB + 2b_0vB = u'B + 2b_0v'B \bmod q,$$

$$[uB + 2b_0vB]_0 = [u'B + 2b_0v'B]_0 \bmod q,$$

$$(u + 2b_0v)b_0 = (u' + 2b_0v')b_0 \bmod q.$$

As $b_0 \neq 0 \bmod q$,

$$(u+2b_0v) =(u'+2b_0v') \bmod q,$$

$$p= u +2b_0v = u' +2b_0v' = p',$$

q.e.d.

Next it is shown that the encrypting function $E(p,X)$ has the property of fully homomorphism.

We simply express above encrypting function such that

$$A_1((\ldots((A_k((M[(A_k^{-1}((\ldots((A_1^{-1}X)Z_1))\ldots))Z_k])Z_k^{-1}))\ldots)) Z_1^{-1})\bmod q$$

$$=A((M[(A^{-1}X)\mathbf{Z}])\mathbf{Z}^{-1})\bmod q.$$

§3.6 Addition/subtraction on ciphertexts

Let

$$M_1:=\mathbf{R}[(u_1\mathbf{1}+v_1B +w_1H)]\mathbf{R}^{-1}\in O,$$

$$M_2:=\mathbf{R}[(u_2\mathbf{1}+v_2B +w_2 H)]\mathbf{R}^{-1}\in O$$

be medium texts to be encrypted where

$$p_1=(u_1+ 2b_0v_1) \bmod q,$$

$$p_2=(u_2+ 2b_0v_2) \bmod q.$$

Let $C_1(X)= E(p_1, X)$ and $C_2(X)= E(p_2, X)$ be the ciphertexts.

$C_1(X)\pm C_2(X) \bmod q =E(p_1,X) \pm E(p_2,X) \bmod q$

$=A_1((\ldots((A_k((M_1[(A_k^{-1}((\ldots((A_1^{-1}X)Z_1))\ldots))Z_k])Z_k^{-1}))\ldots)) Z_1^{-1})$

$\pm A_1((\ldots((A_k((M_2[(A_k^{-1}((\ldots((A_1^{-1}X)Z_1))\ldots))Z_k]) Z_k^{-1}))\ldots)) Z_1^{-1}) \bmod q$

$=A_1((\ldots((A_k(([M_1 \pm M_2] [(A_k^{-1}((\ldots((A_1^{-1}X)Z_1))\ldots))Z_k]) Z_k^{-1}))\ldots)) Z_1^{-1}) \bmod q$

$=A_1((\ldots((A_k(([R(u_1\mathbf{1}+v_1B+w_1H\pm(u_2\mathbf{1}+v_2B+w_2H))R^{-1}]$

$\qquad\qquad [(A_k^{-1}((\ldots((A_1^{-1}X) Z_1))\ldots))Z_k])Z_k^{-1}))\ldots)) Z_1^{-1}) \bmod q$

$=A_1((\ldots((A_k(([R((u_1\pm u_2)\mathbf{1}+(v_1\pm v_2)B+(w_1\pm w_2)H))R^{-1}]$

$\qquad\qquad [(A_k^{-1}((\ldots((A_1^{-1}X)Z_1))\ldots))Z_k]) Z_k^{-1}))\ldots)) Z_1^{-1}) \bmod q$

$= E(p_1\pm p_2,X) \bmod q.$

§3.7 Multiplication on ciphertexts

§3.7.1 Multiplicative property of B and H

We notice multiplication of B and H again where

$$B+H=2b_0\mathbf{1} \bmod q,$$

$$B^2=2b_0B \bmod q,$$

$$H^2=2b_0H \bmod q,$$

$$BH=HB=\mathbf{0} \bmod q.$$

For any $A\in O$, form (11) we have

$$(\mathbf{RBR^{-1}})(\,(\mathbf{RBR^{-1}})\,A) \bmod q$$

$$=(\,(\mathbf{RBR^{-1}})\,(\mathbf{RBR^{-1}}))\,A \bmod q$$

$$=(\mathbf{RB^2R^{-1}})A \bmod q \quad \text{(From Lemma5a)}$$

$$= (2b_0)\,(\mathbf{RBR^{-1}})A \bmod q \qquad\qquad (4.40a)$$

$$(\mathbf{RBR^{-1}})(\,(\mathbf{RHR^{-1}})\,A) \bmod q$$

$$=(\,(\mathbf{RBR^{-1}})\,(\mathbf{R}(2b_0\mathbf{1}\text{-}B)\mathbf{R^{-1}}))\,A \bmod q$$

$$=(2b_0)\,(\,(\mathbf{RBR^{-1}})\,(\mathbf{R1R^{-1}}))\,A\text{-}(\,(\mathbf{RBR^{-1}})\,(\mathbf{RBR^{-1}}))\,A\bmod q$$

$$=(2b_0)(\mathbf{RBR^{-1}})\,A\text{-}\,(2b_0)(\mathbf{RBR^{-1}})\,A\bmod q$$

$$=\mathbf{0} \bmod q \qquad\qquad (4.40b)$$

In the same manner we have

$$(\mathbf{RHR^{-1}})(\,(\mathbf{RHR^{-1}})\,A) \bmod q$$

$$= (2b_0)\,(\mathbf{RHR^{-1}})A \bmod q \qquad\qquad (4.40c)$$

$$(\mathbf{RHR^{-1}})(\,(\mathbf{RBR^{-1}})\,A)=\mathbf{0} \bmod q \qquad\qquad (4.40d)$$

§3.7.2 Multiplication of ciphertexts

Here we consider the multiplicative operation on the ciphertexts.

Let $C_1(X)= E(p_1, X)$ and $C_2(X)= E(p_2, X)$ be the ciphertexts.

$C_1(C_2(X)) \bmod q = E(p_1, E(p_2, X)) \bmod q$

$= A_1((\ldots((A_k((M_1[(A_k^{-1}((\ldots((A_1^{-1}\{A_1((\ldots((A_k((M_2[(A_k^{-1}((\ldots((A_1^{-1}X)Z_1))\ldots))Z_k]) Z_k^{-1}))\ldots))$
$Z_1^{-1}) \})Z_1))\ldots))Z_k]) Z_k^{-1}))\ldots)) Z_1^{-1}) \bmod q$

$= A_1((\ldots((A_k((M_1[M_2[(A_k^{-1}((\ldots((A_1^{-1}X)Z_1))\ldots))Z_k]]) Z_k^{-1}))\ldots)) Z_1^{-1}) \bmod q$

$= A_1((\ldots((A_k(M_1(M_2[(A_k^{-1}((\ldots((A_1^{-1}X)Z_1))\ldots))Z_k]))Z_k^{-1}))\ldots)) Z_1^{-1}) \bmod q.$　　　　(4.41a)

$= A((M_1(M_2[(A^{-1}X)Z]))Z^{-1}) \bmod q.$

Substituting $R (u_1 1 + v_1 B + w_1 H) R^{-1}$, $R (u_2 1 + v_2 B + w_2 H) R^{-1}$ to M_1, M_2 ,

we have from (40a)~(40d)

$= A((\ [R(u_1 1 + v_1 B + w_1 H)R^{-1}]([R (u_2 1 + v_2 B + w_2 H) R^{-1}] [(A^{-1}X)Z]))Z^{-1}) \bmod q,$

$= A((\ [R (u_1 1) R^{-1}]([R(u_2 1 + v_2 B + w_2 H) R^{-1}][(A^{-1}X)Z]))Z^{-1}) \bmod q.$

$+ A((\ [R (v_1 B) R^{-1}] ([R(u_2 1 + v_2 B + w_2 H) R^{-1}][(A^{-1}X)Z]))Z^{-1}) \bmod q$

$+ A((\ [R (w_1 H) R^{-1}] ([R(u_2 1 + v_2 B + w_2 H) R^{-1}] [(A^{-1}X)Z]))Z^{-1}) \bmod.$

$= A((\ [R (u_1 1) R^{-1}]([R(u_2 1) R^{-1}][(A^{-1}X)Z]))Z^{-1}) \bmod q.$

$+ A((\ [R (u_1 1) R^{-1}] ([R (v_2 B) R^{-1}][(A^{-1}X)Z]))Z^{-1}) \bmod q$

$+ A((\ [R (u_1 1) R^{-1}] ([R (w_2 H) R^{-1}][(A^{-1}X)Z]))Z^{-1}) \bmod q$

$+ A((\ [R (v_1 B) R^{-1}]([R (u_2 1) R^{-1}][(A^{-1}X)Z]))Z^{-1}) \bmod q$

$+ A((\ [R (v_1 B) R^{-1}]([R (v_2 B) R^{-1}][(A^{-1}X)Z]))Z^{-1}) \bmod q$

$+ A((\ [R (v_1 B) R^{-1}]([R (w_2 H) R^{-1}][(A^{-1}X)Z]))Z^{-1}) \bmod q$

$+ A(([R (w_1 H) R^{-1}]([R (u_2 1) R^{-1}][(A^{-1}X)Z]))Z^{-1}) \bmod q$

$+ A((([R (w_1 H) R^{-1}]([R (v_2 B) R^{-1}][(A^{-1}X)Z]))Z^{-1}) \bmod q$

$+ A(([R (w_1 H) R^{-1}]([R (w_2 H) R^{-1}][(A^{-1}X)Z]))Z^{-1}) \bmod q$

$= A(([R (u_1 u_2 1 + u_1 v_2 B + u_1 w_2 H + v_1 u_2 B + v_1 v_2 BB + v_1 w_2 BH +$
$w_1 u_2 H + w_1 v_2 HB + w_1 w_2 HH) R^{-1}] [(A^{-1}X)Z]))Z^{-1}) \bmod q$

$= A((([R(u_1 u_2 1 + (u_1 v_2 + v_1 u_2 + 2b_0 v_1 v_2)B + (u_1 w_2 + w_1 u_2 + 2b_0 w_1 w_2)H)R^{-1}]$
$[(A^{-1}X)Z]))Z^{-1}) \bmod q$　　　　(4.41b)

$= A((\ [R(u_1 + v_1 B + w_1 H))R^{-1}](R(u_2 + v_2 B + w_2 H)R^{-1})][(A^{-1}X)Z]))Z^{-1}) \bmod q$

$= A((\ (M_1 M_2) [(A^{-1}X)Z]))Z^{-1}) \bmod q.$

Here we can show that $E(p_1, E(p_2, X))$ mod q is the ciphertext of the multiplication of p_1 and p_2 as follows.

$$p_1 = (u_1 + 2b_0v_1) \bmod q,$$

$$p_2 = (u_2 + 2b_0v_2) \bmod q,$$

$$p_1p_2 = (u_1 + 2b_0v_1)(u_2 + 2b_0v_2) \bmod q,$$

$$= u_1u_2 + 2b_0(v_1u_2 + v_2u_1 + 2b_0v_1v_2) \bmod q.$$

The ciphertext of p_1p_2 is given from definition,

$$E(p_1p_2, X) = A(([R(u^* + v^*B + w^*H)R^{-1})][(A^{-1}X)Z]))Z^{-1}) \bmod q$$

where

$$u^* + 2b_0v^* = p_1p_2 \bmod q,$$

$$w^* \in Fq.$$

From (41a) we have

$$u_1u_2 + 2b_0(u_1v_2 + v_1u_2 + 2b_0v_1v_2) = p_1p_2 \bmod q,$$

$$(u_1w_2 + w_1u_2 + 2b_0w_1w_2) \in Fq.$$

Then we have

$$E(p_1, E(p_2, X)) = E(p_1p_2, X) \bmod q.$$

It has been shown that in this method we have the multiplicative homomorphism on the plaintext p.

§3.8 Property of proposed fully homomorphic encryption

(**IND-CPA security**). Proposed fully homomorphic encryption is **IND-CPA** secure.

As adversary A_d does not know **sk**, A_d is not able to calculate M from the value of $E(u, X)$.

For any PPT adversary A_d it holds that:

$$Adv^{CPA}_{HE}[\lambda] := |Pr[A_d(E(p_0, X)) = 1] - Pr[A_d((E(p_1, X)) = 1]| = negl(\lambda)$$

where **sk** ← **KeyGen**(1^λ).

(**Fully homomorphic encryption**). Proposed fully homomorphic encryption =(**KeyGen; Enc; Dec; Eval**) is fully homomorphic because it satisfies the following properties:

1. Homomorphism: Let $CR = \{CR_\lambda\}_{\lambda \in \mathbb{N}}$ be the set of all polynomial sized arithmetic circuits. On input $\mathbf{sk} \leftarrow \mathbf{KeyGen}(1^\lambda)$, $\forall \text{ckt} \in CR_\lambda$, $\forall (p_1,\ldots,p_n) \in P^n$ where $n = n(\lambda)$, $\forall (C_1,\ldots,C_n)$ where $C_i \leftarrow (E(p_i,X))$, $(i=1,\ldots,n)$, we have $D(\mathbf{sk};\mathbf{Eval}(\text{ckt}; C_1,\ldots,C_n)) = \text{ckt}(p_1,\ldots,p_n)$.

Then it holds that:

$$\Pr[D(\mathbf{sk}; \mathbf{Eval}(\text{ckt}; C_1,\ldots,C_n)) \neq \text{ckt}(p_1,\ldots,p_n)] = \text{negl}(\lambda).$$

2. Compactness: As the output length of **Eval** is at most $k\log_2 q = k\lambda$ where k is a positive integer, there exists a polynomial $\mu = \mu(\lambda)$ such that the output length of **Eval** is at most μ bits long regardless of the input circuit ckt and the number of its inputs.

§4. Analysis of proposed scheme

Here we analyze the proposed fully homomorphism encryption scheme.

§4.1 Computing plaintext p and A_i, Z_i ($i=1,\ldots,k$) from coefficients of ciphertext $E(p,X)$ to be published

Ciphertext $E(p_s,X)$ is published by cloud data centre as follows.

$$E(p_s,X) = A_1((\ldots((A_k((M_s[(A_k^{-1}((\ldots((A_1^{-1}X)Z_1))\ldots))Z_k]))Z_k^{-1}))\ldots)) Z^{-1})$$

$$= A((R[u_s\mathbf{1}+v_sB+w_sH]R^{-1})[(A^{-1}X)Z]))Z^{-1}) \bmod q \in O[X] ,$$

$$= (e_{s00}x_0 + e_{s01}x_1 + \ldots + e_{s07}x_7,$$

$$e_{s10}x_0 + e_{s11}x_1 + \ldots + e_{s17}x_7,$$

$$\ldots \qquad \ldots$$

$$e_{s70}x_0 + e_{s71}x_1 + \ldots + e_{s77}x_7) \quad \bmod q,$$

$$= \{e_{sjk}\}(j,r=0,\ldots,7; s=1,2,3)$$

with $e_{sjt} \in Fq$ $(j,t=0,\ldots,7; s=1,2,3)$ which is published, where

$$p_s = u_s + 2b_0 v_s \bmod q,(s=1,2,3).$$

A_i, Z_i, $R_j \in O$ to be selected randomly such that A_i^{-1}, Z_i^{-1} and R_j^{-1} exist $(i=1,\ldots,k ; j=1,\ldots,r)$ are the secret keys of user A.

We try to find plaintext p_s from coefficients of $E(p_s,X)$, $e_{sjt} \in Fq(j,t=0,\ldots,7;$ $s=1,2,3)$.

In case that $k=8$, $r=8$ and $s=3$ the number of unknown variables $(u_s,v_s,w_s, A_i, Z_i, R_j$ $(k,r=1,\ldots,8;s=1,2,3))$ is $201(=3*3+3*8*8)$, the number of equations is $192(=64*3)$ such that

$$
\left.
\begin{array}{l}
F_{100}(M, A_i, Z_i, R_j)=e_{100} \bmod q, \\[6pt]
F_{101}(M, A_i, Z_i, R_j)=e_{101} \bmod q, \\[6pt]
\quad \cdots \qquad\qquad \cdots \\[6pt]
F_{107}(M, A_i, Z_i, R_j)=e_{107} \bmod q, \\[6pt]
\quad \cdots \qquad\qquad \cdots \\[6pt]
\quad \cdots \qquad\qquad \cdots \\[6pt]
F_{377}(M, A_i, Z_i, R_j)=e_{377} \bmod q,
\end{array}
\right\} \tag{4.42}
$$

where $F_{100},\ldots,F_{377}$ are the $49(=8*2*3+1)^{\text{th}}$ algebraic multivariate equations.

Then the complexity G required for solving above simultaneous equations by using Gröbner basis is given [1.1] such as

$$
G>G'=(_{191+dreg}C_{dreg})^w=(_{4799}C_{191})^w \gg 2^{80}, \tag{4.43}
$$

where G' is the complexity required for solving 192 simultaneous algebraic equations with 191 variables by using Gröbner basis,
where $w=2.39$, and

$$
d_{reg} = 4608 \ (=192*(49-1)/2 - 0\sqrt{}\,(192*(49^2-1)/6)). \tag{4.44}
$$

The complexity G required for solving above simultaneous equations by using Gröbner basis is enough large to be secure.

§4.2 Computing plaintext p_l and d_{ijk} $(i,j,k=0,\ldots,7)$

We try to computing plaintext p_l and d_{ijk} $(i,j,k=0,\ldots,7)$ from coefficients of ciphertext $E(p_l,X)$ to be published.

At first let $E(Y,X) \in O[X,Y]$ be the enciphering function such as

$$
E(Y,X):= A_1((\ldots((A_k((Y[((A_k^{-1}((\ldots((A_1^{-1}X)Z_1))\ldots))Z_k])Z_k^{-1}))\ldots)) Z_1^{-1}) \bmod q \in O[X,Y],
$$

$$
=(d_{000}x_0y_0+d_{001}x_0y_1+ \ldots +d_{077}x_7y_7,
$$

$$
d_{100}x_0y_0+d_{101}x_0y_1+ \ldots +d_{177}x_7y_7,
$$

....

$$d_{700}x_0y_0+d_{701}x_0y_1+ \ldots +d_{777}x_7y_7) \bmod q, \tag{4.45a}$$

$$=\{d_{ijk}\}(i,j,k=0,\ldots,7) \tag{4.45b}$$

with $d_{ijk} \in Fq \ (i,j,k=0,\ldots,7)$.

Next we substitute M_i to Y, where

$$M_i := R[u_i\mathbf{1}+v_iB+w_iH]R^{-1}$$

$$p_i=(u_i+2b_0v_i) \bmod q,$$

$$M_i=(m_{i0},m_{i1},\ldots,m_{i7}) \in O. \tag{4.46}$$

We have

$$E(p_i,X)=A_1((\ldots((A_k((M_i[((A_k^{-1}((\ldots((A_1^{-1}X)Z_1))\ldots))Z_k])Z_k^{-1}))\ldots)) \ Z_1^{-1}) \bmod q \in \quad O[X] ,$$

$$=(d_{000}x_0m_{i0}+d_{001}x_0m_{i1}+ \ldots +d_{077}x_7m_{i7},$$

$$d_{100}x_0m_{i0}+d_{101}x_0m_{i1}+ \ldots +d_{177}x_7m_{i7},$$

....

$$d_{700}x_0m_{i0}+d_{701}x_0m_{i1}+ \ldots +d_{777}x_7m_{i7}) \bmod q, \tag{4.47a}$$

$$=\{d_{ijk}\}(i,j,k=0,\ldots,7) \tag{4.47b}$$

with $d_{ijk} \in Fq \ (i,j,k=0,\ldots,7)$.

Then we obtain 64 equations from (35) and (47a) as follows.

$$\left.\begin{array}{l} d_{000}m_{i0}+d_{001}m_{i1}+ \ldots +d_{007}m_{i7}=e_{00} \\[4pt] d_{010}m_{i0}+d_{011}m_{i1}+ \ldots +d_{017}m_{i7}=e_{01} \\[4pt] \qquad \cdots \qquad\qquad \cdots \\[4pt] d_{070}m_{i0}+d_{071}m_{i1}+ \ldots +d_{077}m_{i7}=e_{07} \end{array}\right\} \tag{4.48a}$$

$$\left.\begin{array}{l} d_{100}m_{i0}+d_{101}m_{i1}+ \ldots +d_{107}m_{i7}=e_{10} \\[4pt] d_{110}m_{i0}+d_{111}m_{i1}+ \ldots +d_{117}m_{i7}=e_{11} \\[4pt] \qquad \cdots \qquad\qquad \cdots \\[4pt] d_{170}m_{i0}+d_{171}m_{i1}+ \ldots +d_{177}m_{i7}=e_{17} \end{array}\right\} \tag{4.48b}$$

....

....

$$d_{700}m_{i0}+d_{701}m_{i1}+ \ldots +d_{707}m_{i7}=e_{70}$$

$$d_{710}m_{i0}+d_{711}m_{i1}+ \ldots +d_{717}m_{i7}=e_{71} \qquad \text{(4.48c)}$$

$$\ldots \qquad \qquad \ldots$$

$$d_{770}m_{i0}+d_{771}m_{i1}+ \ldots +d_{777}m_{i7}=e_{77}$$

For $M_1,\ldots, M_8$ we obtain the same equations, the number of which is 512.
We also obtain the 8 equations such as

$$| E(p_i,\mathbf{1})|^2= |M_i|^2= m_{i0}{}^2+m_{i1}{}^2+\ldots+m_{i7}{}^2 \bmod q,(i=1,\ldots,8). \qquad \text{(4.49)}$$

The number of unknown variables M_i and d_{ijk} $(i,j,k=0,\ldots,7)$ is 576(=512+64).
The number of equations is 520(=512+8).

Then the complexity G required for solving above simultaneous quadratic algebraic equations by using Gröbner basis is given such as

$$G \approx G'=({}_{520+dreg}C_{dreg})^w =({}_{780}C_{260})^w=2^{1699} \quad \gg \quad 2^{80}, \qquad \text{(4.50)}$$

where G' is the complexity required for solving 520 simultaneous quadratic algebraic equations with 519 variables by using Gröbner basis,

where w=2.39,

and

$$d_{reg} = 260(=520*(2-1)/2 - 0\sqrt{\ } (520*(4-1)/6) \qquad \text{(4.51)}$$

It is thought to be difficult computationally to solve the above simultaneous algebraic equations by using Gröbner basis.

§4.3 Attack by using the ciphertexts of p and $-p$

I show that we can not easily distinguish the ciphertexts of p and $-p$.

We try to attack by using "p and $-p$ attack".
We define the medium text M by

$$M:=\mathbf{R}(u\mathbf{1}+v\mathbf{B}+w\mathbf{H})\mathbf{R}^{-1} \in O, \qquad \text{(4.52)}$$

where

a plaintext $p=u+2b_0v \bmod q\in \mathbf{Fq}$, and a random number $w\in \mathbf{Fq}$,

the medium text M. by

$$M_{\cdot}:= R(u'\mathbf{1}+v'B+w'H)R^{-1}\in O, \tag{4.53}$$

where random numbers $u',v',w'\in Fq$ such that

$$-p=u'+2b_0v' \bmod q.$$

By using simple style expression of $E(p, X)$

$$C(X):=E(p, X)= A((M[(A^{-1}X)Z])Z^{-1}) \bmod q \in O[X], \tag{4.54}$$

the ciphertext of $-p$ is defined by

$$C_{\cdot}(X):=E(-p, X)= A(((M_{\cdot}[(A^{-1}X)Z])Z^{-1}) \bmod q \in O[X]. \tag{4.55}$$

$$p=u+2b_0v \bmod q,$$

$$p'=-p=u'+2b_0v' \bmod q,$$

$$p+p'=0=(u+u')+2b_0(v+v').$$

We have

$$C(X)+ C_{\cdot}(X) = E(p, X)+ E(-p, X)= E(p-p, X)= E(0, X)$$

$$=A((\,[M + M_{\cdot}][(A^{-1}X)Z])Z^{-1}) \bmod q$$

$$= (A(\,[R(u\mathbf{1}+vB+wH+u'\mathbf{1}+v'B+w'H)R^{-1}]\,[(A^{-1}X)Z])Z^{-1}) \bmod q$$

$$= (A(\,[R((u+u')\mathbf{1}+(v+v')B+ (w+w')H)R^{-1}]\,[(A^{-1}X)Z])Z^{-1}) \bmod q$$

$$= (A(\,[R((v+v')\,(-2b_0\mathbf{1}+B\,)+ (w+w')H)R^{-1}]\,[(A^{-1}X)Z])Z^{-1}) \bmod q$$

$$= (A(\,[R(-(v+v')\,H+ (w+w')H)R^{-1}]\,[(A^{-1}X)Z])Z^{-1}) \bmod q$$

$$= (A(\,[R(\,(-v-v'+ w+w')H)R^{-1}]\,[(A^{-1}X)Z])Z^{-1}) \bmod q$$

$$\neq \mathbf{0} \bmod q \text{ (in eneral)} \tag{4.56}$$

We can calculate $|C(\mathbf{1})+ C_{\cdot}(\mathbf{1})|^2$ as follows.

Then, from $|H|^2=0 \bmod q$, we have

$$| C(1)+ C.(1) |^2=| E(0, 1)|^2$$

$$= |(A([R((-v-v'+ w+w')H)R^{-1}] [(A^{-1}1)Z])Z^{-1}) |^2 \bmod q$$

$$= | (-v-v'+ w+w')H |^2 \bmod q$$

$$=0 \bmod q.$$

But we can find many M. such that

$$|C(1) + C.(1)|^2=/ A(([M+ M.][(A^{-1}1)Z])Z^{-1}) |^2 =|[M+ M.]|^2 \bmod q,$$

$$=(u+u'+2b_0(v+v'))(u+u'+2b_0(w+w'))$$

$$=0 \bmod q,$$

because we can select many set of u', v' and w' such that

$$u+u'+2b_0(w+w')=0 \bmod q$$

and

$$p+p'= u+u'+2b_0(v+v')\neq 0 \bmod q.$$

That is, even if

$$| C(1)+ C.(1) |^2=0 \bmod q,$$

it does not always hold that

$$p+p' =0 \bmod q.$$

It is said that the attack by using "p and $-p$ attack" is not efficient.

Then we can not easily distinguish the ciphertexts of p and $-p$.

§5. The size of the modulus q and the complexity for enciphering/ deciphering

We consider the size of the system parameter q. We select the size of q such that $O(q)$, the size of the plaintext is larger than 2^{80}. Then we need to select modulus q such as $O(q)=2^{80}$.

In case of $k=8$, $O(q)=2^{80}$, the size of $e_{ij}\in \textbf{\textit{Fq}}$ ($i,j=0,\ldots,7$) which are the coefficients of elements in $E(p,X)=A((M[(A^{-1}X)\textbf{\textit{Z}}])\textbf{\textit{Z}}^{-1})$mod $\in O[X]$ is $(64)(\log_2 q)$bits $=5120$bits, and the size of system parameters q is as large as 80bits.

In case of $k=8$, $O(q)=2^{80}$, the complexity to obtain $E(p,X)$ is

$O(\ (32*512+16*16)(\log_2 q)^2+16*(\ \log_2 q)^3)=2^{27}$ bit-operations,

where $16*16*(\log_2 q)^2+16*(\ \log_2 q)^3$ is the complexiy for inverse of A^{-1} and $\textbf{\textit{Z}}^{-1}$.

And the complexity required for deciphering is given as follows.
Let $C:=A_1((\ldots((A_k((M[(A_k^{-1}((\ldots((A_1^{-1}\textbf{1})Z_1))\ldots))Z_k])\ Z_k^{-1}))\ldots))\ Z_1^{-1})$ mod q.
We have

$$(A_k\ ((\ldots((A_1^{-1}\ C\ )Z_1))\ Z_2))\ldots))Z_k =M[(A_k^{-1}((\ldots((A_1^{-1}\textbf{1})Z_1))\ldots))Z_k]\ mod\ q,$$

$$M=[(A_k\ ((\ldots((A_1^{-1}\ C\ )Z_1))\ Z_2))\ldots))\ Z_k][(A_k^{-1}((\ldots((A_1^{-1}\textbf{1})Z_1))\ldots))Z_k]^{-1}mod\ q.$$

$$=R_1(\ldots(R_r(u\textbf{1}+vB+w\ H)R_r^{-1})\ldots)R_1^{-1}$$

$$M'=(m_0',m_1',\ldots,m_7'):=(u\textbf{1}+vB+w\ H)=R_r^{-1}\ (\ldots(R_1^{-1}M\ R_1)\ldots)\ R_r$$

$$p=[M'B]_0/b_0\ mod\ q.$$

Then the complexity G is

$O(\ (16*64+15*64+16*64+2)(\log_2 q)^2+(1+8)*[8*(\log_2 q)^2+(\log_2 q)^3]$

$+9*(\log_2 q)^2+(\ \log_2 q)^3)$

$=O(\ (3091)(\log_2 q)^2+(10)(\ \log_2 q)^3)=2^{25}$ bit-operations.

On the other hand the complexity of the enciphering and deciphering in RSA scheme is

$O(2(\log n)^3)=2^{34}$ bit-operations

where the size of modulus n is 2048bits.

Then our scheme requires small memory space and complexity to encipher and decipher so that we are able to implement our scheme to the mobile device.

§6. Conclusion of chapter 4

We proposed the new fully homomorphism encryption scheme based on the octonion ring over finite field that requires small memory space and complexity to encipher and decipher. It was shown that our scheme is immune from the Gröbner basis attacks by calculating the complexity to obtain the Gröbner basis for the multivariate algebraic equations and immune from "p and -p attack".

The proposed scheme does not require a "bootstrapping" process so that the complexity to encipher and decipher is not large.

§7.Acknowledgments

This paper is the revised chapter 4 of my work "Fully Homomorphic Encryption without bootstrapping" published in March, 2015 which was published by LAP LAMBERT Academic Publishing, Saarbrücken/Germany [0.3].

I would like to thankYongge Wang for some discussion on the scheme [0.5].

【Explanation of the figure】

　【Fig.1】　The conceptual chart of additional circuit of ciphertexts

　　【Explanation on symbol】

　　1 1 0 ...ciphertext of plaintext p_1

　　1 2 0 ...ciphertext of plaintext p_2

　　1 3 0 ...additional circuit

　　1 4 0 ...ciphertext of plaintext p_1+p_2

　【Fig.2】　The conceptual chart of multiplicative circuit of ciphertexts

　　【Explanation on symbol】

　　2 1 0 ...ciphertext of plaintext p_1

　　2 2 0 ...ciphertext of plaintext p_2

　　2 3 0 ...multiplicative circuit

　　2 4 0 ...ciphertext of plaintext $p_1 p_2$

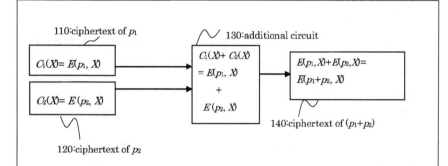

110:ciphertext of p_1

130:additional circuit

$C_1(X) = E(p_1, X)$

$C_2(X) = E(p_2, X)$

$C_1(X) + C_2(X)$
$= E(p_1, X)$
$+$
$E(p_2, X)$

$E(p_1, X) + E(p_2, X) =$
$E(p_1 + p_2, X)$

140:ciphertext of $(p_1 + p_2)$

120:ciphertext of p_2

Fig.1　The conceptual chart of additional circuit of ciphertexts

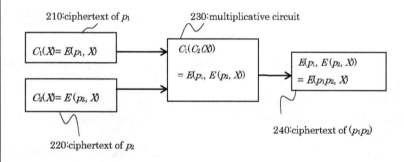

210:ciphertext of p_1

230:multiplicative circuit

$C_1(X) = E(p_1, X)$

$C_2(X) = E(p_2, X)$

$C_1(C_2(X))$
$= E(p_1, E(p_2, X))$

$E(p_1, E(p_2, X))$
$= E(p_1 p_2, X)$

240:ciphertext of $(p_1 p_2)$

220:ciphertext of p_2

Fig.2 The conceptual chart of multiplicative circuit of ciphertexts

BIBLIOGRAPHY

[0.1] Craig Gentry. Fully Homomorphic Encryption Using Ideal Lattices.In the 41st ACM Symposium on Theory of Computing (STOC), 2009.

[0.2] John H. Conway, Derek A. Smith co-authored, translated by Syuuji Yamada, "On Quaternions and Octonions " Baifuukan Publication Center, Tokyo, .2006.

[0.3] Masahiro, Y. (2015). Fully Homomorphic Encryption without bootstrapping. Saarbrücken/Germany: LAP LAMBERT Academic Publishing.

[0.4] Mashiro Yagisawa," Fully Homomorphic Encryption without bootstrapping", Cryptology ePrint Archive, Report 2015/474, 2015. http://eprint.iacr.org/.

[0.5] Yongge Wang," Notes on Two Fully Homomorphic Encryption Schemes Without Bootstrapping", Cryptology ePrint Archive, Report 2015/519, 2015. http://eprint.iacr.org/.

[1.1] M. Bardet, J. C. Faugere, and B. Salvy, "On the complexity of Gröbner basis computation of semi-regular overdetermined algebraic equations," Proceeding of the International Conference on Polynomial System   Solving(ICPSS2004), pp.71-75, November 2004.

[2.1] R. L. Rivest, L. Adleman, and M. L. Dertouzos.   On data banks and privacy homomorphisms.   In Foundations of Secure Computation, 1978.

[2.2] http://www-03.ibm.com/press/us/en/pressrelease/27840.wss

[2.3] Michael Cooney (2009-06-25). ""IBM touts encryption innovation". Computer World. Retrieved 2009-07-14.

[2.4] Damien Stehle; Ron Steinfeld (2010-05-19). "Faster Fully Homomorphic Encryption" (PDF). International Association for Cryptologic Research. Retrieved 2010-09-15.

[2.5] Craig Gentry, A Fully Homomorphic Encryption Scheme, 2009.   Available at http://crypto.stanford.edu/craig/craig-thesis.pdf .

[2.6] Craig Gentry. "Computing Arbitrary Functions of Encrypted Data". Association for Computing Machinery.

[2.7] Marten van Dijk; Craig Gentry, Shai Halevi, and Vinod Vaikuntanathan (2009-12-11). "Fully Homomorphic Encryption over the Integers" (PDF). International Association for Cryptologic Research. Retrieved 2010-03-18.

[2.8] Bram Cohen. "Simple Public Key Encryption".   Available at http://en.wikipedia.org/wiki/Cohen's_cryptosystem .

[2.9] JS Coron, A Mandal, D Naccache, M Tibouchi ," Fully homomorphic encryption over the integers with shorter public keys", Advances in Cryptology–CRYPTO 2011, 487-504.

[2.10] Halevi, Shai. "An Implementation of homomorphic encryption". Retrieved 30 April 2013. Available at https://github.com/shaih/HElib .

[2.11] Nuida and Kurosawa,"(Batch) Fully Homomorphic Encryption over Integers for Non-Binary Message Spaces", Cryptology ePrint Archive, Report 2014/777, 2014. http://eprint.iacr.org/.

[4.1] Shigeo Tsujii , Kohtaro Tadaki , Masahito Gotaishi ,Ryo Fujita ,and Masao Kasahara ,"Proposal Integrated MPKC:PPS—STS Enhanced Perturbed Piece in Hand Method---," IEICE Tech. Rep.ISEC2009-27,SITE2009-19,ICSS2009-41(2009-07),July 2009.

[4.2] S. Tsujii, K. Tadaki, and R. Fujita, "Piece in hand concept for enhancing the security of multivariate type public key cryptosystems: Public key without containing all the information of secret key," Cryptology ePrint Archive, Report 2004/366, 2004.

[4.3] C.Wolf, and B. Preneel, "Taxonomy of public key schemes based on the problem of multivariate quadratic equations," Cryptology ePrint Archive, Report 2005/077, 2005, http://eprint.iacr.org/.

Appendix A:

Octinv(*A*) --

$S \leftarrow a_0^2 + a_1^2 + \ldots + a_7^2$ mod q.

% S^{-1} mod q

    q[1] ← q div S ;% integer part of q/S

    r[1] ← q mod S ;% residue

    k ← 1

    q[0] ← q

    r[0] ← S

    while r[k] ≠ 0

      begin

        k ← k + 1

        q[k] ← r[k−2] div r[k−1]

        r[k] ← r[k−2] mod [rk−1]

      end

Q [k−1] ← (-1)*q[k−1]

L[k−1] ← 1

i ← k−1

while   i > 1

    begin

      Q[i−1] ← (-1)*Q[i] *q[i−1] + L[i]

      L[i−1] ← Q[i]

      i ← i−1

    end

invS ← Q[1] mod q

invA[0] ← a_0*invS mod q

For i=1,…,7,

    invA[i] ← (-1)*a_i*invS mod q

Return A^{-1} = (invA[0], invA[1],…, invA[7])

Appendix B:

Theorem 4.1

Let $A=(a_{10},a_{11},...,a_{17})\in O$, $a_{1j}\in \boldsymbol{Fq}$ $(j=0,1,...,7)$.

Let $A^n=(a_{n0},a_{n1},...,a_{n7})\in O$, $a_{nj}\in \boldsymbol{Fq}$ $(n=1,...,7;j=0,1,...,7)$.

a_{00}, a_{nj}'s$(n=1,2,...;j=0,1,...)$and b_n's $(n=0,1,...)$ satisfy the equations such that

$N= a_{11}^2+...+a_{17}^2 \bmod q$

$a_{00}=1$, $b_0=0$, $b_1=1$,

$a_{n0}= a_{n-1,0}\,a_{10} - b_{n-1}N \bmod q$,$(n=1,2,...)$ (4.8)

$b_n= a_{n-1,0}+ b_{n-1}a_{10} \bmod q$,$(n=1,2,...)$ (4.9)

$a_{nj}= b_n a_{1j} \bmod q$,$(n=1,2,...;j=1,2,...,7)$.   (4.10)

(*Proof:*)

We use mathematical induction method.

[step 1]

When $n=1$, (4.8) holds because

$a_{10}= a_{00}\,a_{10} - b_0N=a_{10} \bmod q$.

(4.9) holds because

$b_1= a_{00}+ b_0a_{10} =a_{00} =1\bmod q$.

(4.10) holds because

$a_{1j}= b_1a_{1j} = a_{1j} \bmod q$,$(j=1,2,...,7)$

[step 2]

When $n=k$,

If it holds that

$a_{k0}= a_{k-1,0}\,a_{10} - b_{k-1}N \bmod q$,$(k=2,3,4,...)$,

$b_k= a_{k-1,0}+ b_{k-1}a_{10} \bmod q$,

$a_{kj}= b_k a_{1j} \bmod q$,$(j=1,2,...,7)$,

from (4.9)

$b_{k-1}= a_{k-2,0}+ b_{k-2}a_{10} \bmod q$,$(k=2,3,4,...)$,

then

$A^{k+1}=A^kA=(a_{k0}, b_k a_{11},..., b_k a_{17})(a_{10},a_{11},...,a_{17})$

$=(a_{k0}\,a_{10} - b_kN, a_{k0}\,a_{11}+ b_k a_{11}\,a_{10},..., a_{k0}\,a_{17}+ b_k a_{17}\,a_{10})$

$=(a_{k0}\,a_{10} - b_kN, (a_{k0} + b_k a_{10})a_{11},..., (a_{k0} + b_k a_{10})a_{17})$

$=(a_{k+1,0}, b_{k+1,0}\,a_{11},..., b_{k+1,0}\,a_{17})$,

as was required.   q.e.d.

Appendix C:

Theorem 4.2

For an element $A=(a_{10}, a_{11}, ..., a_{17}) \in O$,

$A^{J+1}=A \bmod q$,

where

$J := LCM \{q^2-1, q-1\} = q^2-1$,

$N := a_{11}^2 + a_{12}^2 + ... + a_{17}^2 \neq 0 \bmod q$.

(*Proof:*)

From (4.8) and (4.9) it comes that

$a_{n0} = a_{n-1,0} a_{10} - b_{n-1} N \bmod q$,

$b_n = a_{n-1,0} + b_{n-1} a_{10} \bmod q$,

$a_{n0} a_{10} + b_n N = (a_{n-1,0} a_{10} - b_{n-1} N) a_{10} + (a_{n-1,0} + b_{n-1} a_{10}) N = a_{n-1,0} a_{10}^2 + a_{n-1,0} N \bmod q$,

$b_n N = a_{n-1,0} a_{10}^2 + a_{n-1,0} N - a_{n0} a_{10} \bmod q$,

$b_{n-1} N = a_{n-2,0} a_{10}^2 + a_{n-2,0} N - a_{n-1,0} a_{10} \bmod q$,

$a_{n0} = 2 a_{10} a_{n-1,0} - (a_{10}^2 + N) a_{n-2,0} \bmod q$, $(n=1,2,...)$.

1) In case that $-N \neq 0 \bmod q$ is quadratic non-residue of prime q,

Because $-N \neq 0 \bmod q$ is quadratic non-residue of prime q,

$(-N)^{(q-1)/2} = -1 \bmod q$.

$a_{n0} - 2 a_{10} a_{n-1,0} + (a_{10}^2 + N) a_{n-2,0} = 0 \bmod q$,

$a_{n0} = (\beta^n(a_{10}-\alpha) + (\beta - a_{10})\alpha^n)/(\beta - \alpha)$ over $Fq[\alpha]$

$b_n = (\beta^n - \alpha^n)/(\beta - \alpha)$ over $Fq[\alpha]$

where α, β are roots of algebraic quadratic equation such that

$t^2 - 2a_{10}t + a_{10}^2 + N = 0$.

$\alpha = a_{10} + \sqrt{-N}$ over $Fq[\alpha]$,

$\beta = a_{10} - \sqrt{-N}$ *over Fq[α].*

We can calculate β^{q^2} as follows.

$$\beta^{q^2} = (a_{10} - \sqrt{-N})^{q^2} \quad over\ Fq[\alpha]$$

$$= (a_{10}{}^q - \sqrt{-N}(-N)^{(q-1)/2})^q \ over\ Fq[\alpha]$$

$$= (a_{10} \quad - \sqrt{-N}(-N)^{(q-1)/2})^q \ over\ Fq[\alpha]$$

$$= (a_{10}{}^q - \sqrt{-N}(-N)^{(q-1)/2}(-N)^{(q-1)/2}) \ over\ Fq[\alpha]$$

$$= a_{10} \quad - \sqrt{-N}(-1)(-1) \quad over\ \boldsymbol{Fq}[\alpha]$$

$$= a_{10} - \sqrt{-N} \ over\ \boldsymbol{Fq}[\alpha]$$

$$= \beta \ over\ Fq[\alpha].$$

In the same manner we obtain

$$\alpha^{q^2} = \alpha\ over\ \boldsymbol{Fq}[\alpha].$$

$$a_{q^2,0} = (\beta^{q^2}(a_{10} - \alpha) + (\beta - a_{10})\alpha^{q^2})/(\beta - \alpha)$$

$$=(\beta(a_{10}\text{-}\alpha) + (\beta\text{-}a_{10})\alpha)/(\beta\text{-}\alpha)=a_{10}\ \bmod q.$$

$$b_{q^2} = (\beta^{q^2} - \alpha^{q^2})/(\beta - \alpha) = 1\ \bmod q.$$

Then we obtain

$$A^{q2}=(a_{q2,0},b_{q2}a_{11},...,b_{q2}a_{17})$$

$$=(\ a_{10},\ a_{11},...,a_{17})=A\ \bmod q$$

2) In case that $-N \neq 0 \bmod q$ is quadratic residue of prime q

$$a_{n0}=(\beta^n(a_{10}\text{-}\alpha) + (\beta\text{-}a_{10})\alpha^n)/(\beta\text{-}\alpha) \quad \bmod q,$$

$$b_{n0}=(\beta^n\text{-}\alpha^n)/(\beta\text{-}\alpha) \quad \bmod q ,$$

As $\alpha,\beta \in \boldsymbol{Fq},$ from Fermat's little Theorem

$\beta^q = \beta \bmod q$,

$\alpha^q = \alpha \bmod q$.

Then we have

$a_{q0} = (\beta^q(a_{10}-\alpha) + (\beta - a_{10})\alpha^q)/(\beta - \alpha) \bmod q$

$= (\beta(a_{10}-\alpha) + (\beta - a_{10})\alpha)/(\beta - \alpha) \bmod q$

$= a_{10} \bmod q$

$b_q = (\beta^q - \alpha^q)/(\beta - \alpha) = 1 \bmod q$.

Then we have

$a^q = (a_{q0}, b_q a_{11}, \dots, b_q a_{17})$

$= (a_{10}, a_{11}, \dots, a_{17}) = a \bmod q$.

We therefore arrive at the equation such as

$A^{J+1} = A \bmod q$ for arbitrary element $A \in O$, where

$J = \mathrm{LCM}\{q^2-1, q-1\} = q^2-1$,

as was required.   q.e.d.

We notice that

in case that $-N = 0 \bmod q$

$a_{00} = 1$, $b_0 = 0$, $b_1 = 1$,

From (4.8)

$a_{n0} = a_{n-1,0} a_{10} \bmod q$, $(n=1,2,\dots)$,

then we have

$a_{n0} = a_{10}{}^n \bmod q$, $(n=1,2,\dots)$.

$a_{q0} = a_{10}{}^q = a_{10} \bmod q$.

From (4.9),

$b_n = a_{n-1,0} + b_{n-1}a_{10} \bmod q$,$(n=1,2,\ldots)$

$= a_{10}{}^{n-1} + b_{n-1}a_{10} \bmod q$

$= 2a_{10}{}^{n-1} + b_{n-2}a_{10}^2 \bmod q$

$\ldots \qquad \ldots$

$= (n-1)a_{10}{}^{n-1} + b_1 a_{10}{}^{n-1} \bmod q$

$= na_{10}{}^{n-1} \bmod q.$

Then we have

$a_{nj} = na_{10}{}^{n-1}a_{1j} \bmod q$,$(n=1,2,\ldots;j=1,2,\ldots,7)$.

$a_{qj} = qa_{10}{}^{q-1}a_{1j} \bmod q = 0, (j=1,2,\ldots,7)$.

Appendix D:

Lemma 4.2

$$A^{-1}(AB)= B$$
$$(BA)A^{-1}= B$$

(*Proof:*)

$A^{-1}= (a_0/|A|^2 \bmod q, -a_1/|A|^2 \bmod q,\ldots, -a_7/|A|^2 \bmod q)$.

$AB \bmod q$

$= (a_0b_0-a_1b_1- a_2b_2- a_3b_3-a_4b_4- a_5b_5-a_6b_6-a_7b_7 \bmod q,$

$a_0b_1+a_1b_0+a_2b_4+a_3b_7-a_4b_2+a_5b_6-a_6b_5-a_7b_3 \bmod q,$

$a_0b_2-a_1b_4+a_2b_0+a_3b_5+a_4b_1-a_5b_3+a_6b_7-a_7b_6 \bmod q,$

$a_0b_3-a_1b_7-a_2b_5+a_3b_0+a_4b_6+a_5b_2-a_6b_4+a_7b_1 \bmod q,$

$a_0b_4+a_1b_2-a_2b_1-a_3b_6+a_4b_0+a_5b_7+a_6b_3-a_7b_5 \bmod q,$

$a_0b_5-a_1b_6+a_2b_3-a_3b_2-a_4b_7+a_5b_0+a_6b_1+a_7b_4 \bmod q,$

$a_0b_6+a_1b_5-a_2b_7+a_3b_4-a_4b_3-a_5b_1+a_6b_0+a_7b_2 \bmod q,$

$a_0b_7+a_1b_3+a_2b_6-a_3b_1+a_4b_5-a_5b_4-a_6b_2+a_7b_0 \bmod q)$.

$[A^{-1}(AB)]_0$

$=\{ a_0(a_0b_0-a_1b_1- a_2b_2- a_3b_3-a_4b_4- a_5b_5-a_6b_6-a_7b_7)$

$+a_1(a_0b_1+a_1b_0+a_2b_4+a_3b_7-a_4b_2+a_5b_6-a_6b_5-a_7b_3)$

$+ a_2(a_0b_2-a_1b_4+a_2b_0+a_3b_5+a_4b_1-a_5b_3+a_6b_7-a_7b_6)$

$+a_3(a_0b_3-a_1b_7-a_2b_5+a_3b_0+a_4b_6+a_5b_2-a_6b_4+a_7b_1)$

$+a_4(a_0b_4+a_1b_2-a_2b_1-a_3b_6+a_4b_0+a_5b_7+a_6b_3-a_7b_5)$

$+ a_5(a_0b_5-a_1b_6+a_2b_3-a_3b_2-a_4b_7+a_5b_0+a_6b_1+a_7b_4)$

$+a_6(a_0b_6+a_1b_5-a_2b_7+a_3b_4-a_4b_3-a_5b_1+a_6b_0+a_7b_2)$

$+a_7(a_0b_7+a_1b_3+a_2b_6-a_3b_1+a_4b_5-a_5b_4-a_6b_2+a_7b_0)\} /|A|^2 \bmod q$

$=\{(a_0^2+a_1^2+\ldots +a_7^2) b_0\} /|A|^2 =b_0 \bmod q$

where $[M]_n$ denotes the n-th element of $M\in O$.

$[A^{-1}(AB)]_1$

$$=\{ a_0(a_0b_1+a_1b_0+a_2b_4+a_3b_7-a_4b_2+a_5b_6-a_6b_5-a_7b_3)$$

$$-a_1(a_0b_0-a_1b_1- a_2b_2- a_3b_3-a_4b_4- a_5b_5-a_6b_6-a_7b_7)$$

$$-a_2(a_0b_4+a_1b_2-a_2b_1-a_3b_6+a_4b_0+a_5b_7+a_6b_3-a_7b_5)$$

$$-a_3(a_0b_7+a_1b_3+a_2b_6-a_3b_1+a_4b_5-a_5b_4-a_6b_2+a_7b_0)$$

$$+a_4(a_0b_2-a_1b_4+a_2b_0+a_3b_5+a_4b_1-a_5b_3+a_6b_7-a_7b_6)$$

$$- a_5(a_0b_6+a_1b_5-a_2b_7+a_3b_4-a_4b_3-a_5b_1+a_6b_0+a_7b_2)$$

$$+a_6(a_0b_5-a_1b_6+a_2b_3-a_3b_2-a_4b_7+a_5b_0+a_6b_1+a_7b_4)$$

$$+a_7(a_0b_3-a_1b_7-a_2b_5+a_3b_0+a_4b_6+a_5b_2-a_6b_4+a_7b_1)\} /|A|^2 \bmod q$$

$$=\{(a_0^2+a_1^2+\ldots+a_7^2)\, b_1\} /|A|^2 = b_1 \bmod q.$$

Similarly we have

$[A^{-1}(AB)]_i = b_1 \bmod q$ (i=2,3,…,7).

Then

$$A^{-1}(AB)= B \bmod q. \qquad \text{q.e.d.}$$

www.ingramcontent.com/pod-product-compliance
Lightning Source LLC
LaVergne TN
LVHW042345060326
832902LV00006B/405